KNIT IT!
WEAR IT!

Bobbie Matela, Managing Editor

Carol Wilson Mansfield, Art Director

Mary Ann Frits, Editorial Director

Kelly Robinson, Sandy Scoville, and Kathy Wesley, Editorial Staff

Kathryn Smith, Assistant Editor

Graphic Solutions inc-chgo, Book Design

Patterns tested and models made by Mary Ann Frits, Pat Hyland, Dolores Roberts, Sandy Scoville, Rita Weiss, and Kathy Wesley.

For a full-color catalog including books of crochet and knit designs, write to:

American School of Needlework®
Consumer Division
1455 Linda Vista Drive
San Marcos, CA 92069

We have made every effort to ensure the accuracy and completeness of these instructions. We cannot, however, be responsible for human error, typographical mistakes, or variations in individual work.

Introduction

No one in your household will be left out in the cold when you explore this treasury of favorite family fashions to knit and wear.

This array of diverse patterns includes gloves, socks, mittens, sweaters and scarves; also babies' sweaters and booties, children's sweaters (with a matching sweater for Teddy), and—in case your dog is a clotheshorse—a cute canine coat, too!

Even beginners can knit with confidence, using the complete and easy-to-follow instructions provided with each project. These designs are crafted in a variety of yarns and a wide range of colors to inspire creativity in every knitter.

Discover stylish solutions for all your gift-giving woes: *everyone* appreciates a handcrafted gift—especially a garment that will envelop the recipient in your loving touch. What's more, any needleworker on your gift list will delight in receiving this most comprehensive guide for creating fashionable knitwear.

So don't leave this book sitting around unless you're prepared for all the requests that are bound to come your way—you may never get a chance to make that special sweater that would look so nice on *you*!

Abbreviations and Symbols

beg	begin(ning)
CB	cable back
CF	cable front
inc	increase(-ing)
K	knit
P	purl
K2 tog	knit 2 together
P2 tog	purl 2 together
patt	pattern
prev	previous
PSSO	pass slipped stitch over
PSSO2	pass slipped stitch over 2
rem	remain(ing)
rep	repeat(ing)
rnd(s)	round(s)
sl	slip
st(s)	stitch(es)
stock st	stockinette stitch
tbl	through back loop
tog	together
yb	yarn back
yf	yarn front
YO	yarn over

* An asterisk (or double asterisk ******) is used to mark the beginning of a portion of instructions to be worked more than once; thus, "rep from ***** twice more" means after working the instructions once, repeat the instructions following the asterisk twice more (3 times in all).

— The number after a long dash at the end of a row or round indicates the number of stitches you should have when the row or round has been completed.

( ) Parentheses are used to enclose instructions which should be worked the exact number of times specified immediately following the parentheses, such as "(K2, P2) twice."

( ) Parentheses are also used to provide additional information to clarify instructions.

Terms

Right or Wrong?
We use these words in several different ways.

Right Side of the garment means the side that will be seen when it is worn.

Wrong Side of the garment means the side that will be inside when it is worn.

Right Front means the part of the garment that will be worn on the right front.

Left Front means the part of the garment that will be worn on the left front.

Continue in Pattern as Established is usually used in a pattern stitch, and this means to continue following the pattern stitch as it is already set up (established) on the needle, working any subsequent increases or decreases (usually, worked at the beginning or end of a row) in such a way that the established pattern remains the same.

Work Even means to continue to work in the pattern as established, without working any increases or decreases.

An Important Word About Gauge

A correct stitch gauge is very important. Please take the time to work a stitch gauge swatch about 4" x 4". Measure the swatch. If the number of stitches and rows are fewer than indicated under "Gauge" in the pattern, your needles are too large. Try another swatch with smaller size needles. If the number of stitches and rows are more than indicated under "Gauge" in the pattern, your needles are too small. Try another swatch with larger size needles.

Metric Conversion Charts

INCHES INTO MILLIMETERS & CENTIMETERS (Rounded off slightly)

inches	mm	cm	inches	cm	inches	cm	inches	cm
1/8	3		5	12.5	21	53.5	38	96.5
1/4	6		5 1/2	14	22	56	39	99
3/8	10	1	6	15	23	58.5	40	101.5
1/2	13	1.3	7	18	24	61	41	104
5/8	15	1.5	8	20.5	25	63.5	42	106.5
3/4	20	2	9	23	26	66	43	109
7/8	22	2.2	10	25.5	27	68.5	44	112
1	25	2.5	11	28	28	71	45	114.5
1 1/4	32	3.2	12	30.5	29	73.5	46	117
1 1/2	38	3.8	13	33	30	76	47	119.5
1 3/4	45	4.5	14	35.5	31	79	48	122
2	50	5	15	38	32	81.5	49	124.5
2 1/2	65	6.5	16	40.5	33	84	50	127
3	75	7.5	17	43	34	86.5		
3 1/2	90	9	18	46	35	89		
4	100	10	19	48.5	36	91.5		
4 1/2	115	11.5	20	51	37	94		

mm - millimeter   cm - centimeter

KNITTING NEEDLES CONVERSION CHART

U.S.	0	1		2		3	4	5		6	7	8	9	10	10 1/2			11	13	15
Metric(mm)	2	2 1/4	2 1/2	2 3/4	3	3 1/4	3 1/2	3 3/4	4		4 1/2	5	5 1/2	6	6 1/2	7	7 1/2	8	9	10
U.K.	14	13		12	11	10		9	8		7	6	5	4	3	2	1	0	00	000

5

Special Techniques

Weaving On Two Needles—Kitchener Stitch

This method of weaving is used for garments which have been knitted in stockinette stitch, and which require joining without a seam, such as the toe of a sock.

To weave the edges together and form an unbroken line of stockinette stitch, divide all stitches evenly onto two knitting needles - one behind the other.

Thread yarn into tapestry needle; with wrong sides together, work from right to left as follows:

Step 1:
Insert tapestry needle into the first stitch on the front needle as to purl (**Fig 1**). Draw yarn through stitch, leaving stitch on knitting needle.

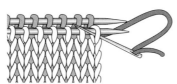
Fig 1

Step 2:
Insert tapestry needle into the first stitch on the back needle as to purl (**Fig 2**). Draw yarn through stitch and slip stitch off knitting needle.

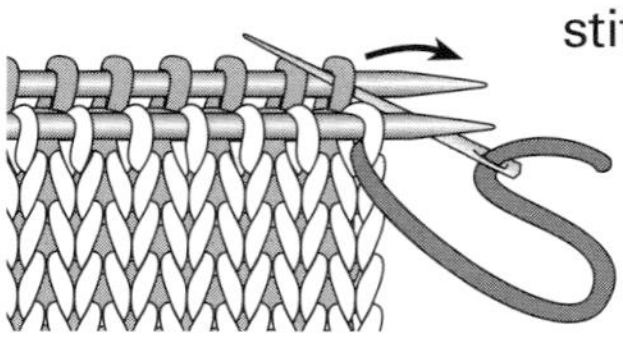

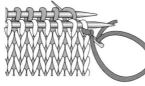
Fig 2

Step 3:
Insert tapestry needle into the next stitch on same (back) needle as to knit (**Fig 3**), leaving stitch on knitting needle.

Fig 3

Step 4:
Insert tapestry needle into the first stitch on the front needle as to knit (**Fig 4**). Draw yarn through stitch and slip stitch off knitting needle.

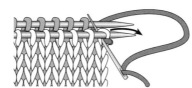
Fig 4

Step 5:
Insert tapestry needle into the next stitch on same (front) needle as to purl (**Fig 5**). Draw yarn through stitch, leaving stitch on knitting needle.

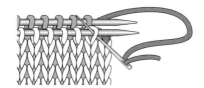
Fig 5

Repeat Steps 2 through 5 until one stitch is left on each needle. Then repeat Steps 2 and 4. Finish off.

Hint: When weaving, do not pull yarn tightly or too loosely; woven stitches should be the same size as adjacent knitted stitches.

Knitting With Double-Pointed Needles

Some of the projects in this book are made using a set of four double-pointed needles. To work with double-pointed needles, divide stitches onto 3 needles as instructed in specific pattern. Join by inserting the 4th needle into the first stitch (**Fig 6**), being careful not to twist the stitches, and work this stitch. After working all the stitches off a needle, use the free needle to work the stitches off the next needle. Continue in this manner, being sure to pull the yarn tightly across to the first stitch of each needle to avoid loose stitches.

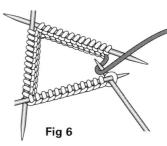
Fig 6

GALLERY OF PROJECTS

Design Directory

	Pattern	Color Photograph
For Men		
Casual Elegance	18	front cover & 12
Handsome Fisherman	32	13
Heather Cables	35	12
For Women		
Country Weekend for Her	22	front cover & 11
Feminine Touch	27	13
Flirty Scarf	30	9
Gloves for Her	30	back cover
Heather Stripe Knee Socks	37	11
Heavenly	38	9
Leafy Stripes	47	10
Northern Lights Mittens	54	back cover
Saturday Stripes Socks	61	10
Spirited Stripes	65	front cover & back cover
Sporty Cuffed Socks	67	10
Winter Day Knee Socks	69	11
Winter Warmth	73	9
For Children		
Country Weekend for Kids	24	front cover & 11
Honey It's Cold!	39	back cover
In Vest for Kids	44	16
Snowtime Mittens	62	back cover
Young Fisherman Set	74	16
For Babies		
Blue Skies	17	front cover & 15
Just Ducky	46	15
Let's Go Visiting	49	15
Playtime for Baby	56	14
So Sweet	64	front cover & 15
What A Hoot! Baby Sweater	70	14
For Furry Friends		
Country Weekend for Teddy	26	front cover & 11
Hound's Check	42	front cover &16

Heavenly

Winter Warmth

Flirty Scarf

9

Leafy Stripes

Saturday Stripe Socks

Sporty Cuffed Socks

Country Weekend Sweaters

Country Weekend for Her

Country Weekend for Kids

Country Weekend for Teddy

Winter Day Knee Socks

Heather Stripe Knee Socks

Heather Cables

Casual Elegance

12

Feminine Touch

Handsome
Fisherman

13

**What A Hoot !
Baby Sweater**

**Playtime
for Baby**

14

So Sweet

Blue Skies

Just Ducky

Let's Go Visiting

15

Young Fisherman Set

In Vest for Kids

Hound's Check

16

Blue Skies

Keep baby's tootsies warm and protected with this sweet pair of blue booties.

Size:
About 4" from heel to toe

Materials:
Baby weight yarn, 1 oz (170 yds, 30 g) blue; 12 yds white

Size 3 straight knitting needles, or size required for gauge

Size 7 straight knitting needles

2 small stitch holders

Size 18 tapestry needle

One yd ³/₈"-wide white satin ribbon

Gauge:
With smaller size needles, 15 sts = 2" in garter stitch (knit every row)

Instructions

Bootie (make 2)

Starting at top edge with larger size needles and blue, cast on 41 sts.

Row 1 (right side):
P1; * yb, sl 1 as to purl; yf, P1; rep from * across.

Row 2:
Purl.

Rows 3 through 8:
Rep Rows 1 and 2, 3 times.

Note: Change color by bringing new color under old color to prevent holes. Unless otherwise indicated, carry unused color along side.

Join white. Rep Rows 1 and 2 in following stripe pattern:

- ❑ white, 6 rows
- ❑ blue, 8 rows
- ❑ white, 6 rows
- ❑ blue, 6 rows

Cut white. Change to smaller size needles.

Ribbing:
Row 1 (right side):
With blue, K1; * P1, K1; rep from * across.

Row 2:
P1; * K1, P1; rep from * across.

Row 3 (beading row):
K1; * YO, K2 tog; rep from * across.

Row 4:
Rep Row 2. At end of row—41 sts.

Instep:
Row 1 (right side):
* K1, P1; rep from * 13 times more; sl rem 13 sts onto a stitch holder.

Row 2:
K1; * P1, K1; rep from * 6 times more; sl rem 13 sts onto a stitch holder.

Row 3:
P1; * K1, P1; rep from * 6 times more.

Row 4:
K1; * P1, K1; rep from * 6 times more.

Rep Rows 3 and 4 until instep measures 1³/₄" long, ending by working a Row 4.

Cut yarn, leaving sts on needle.

Foot:
With right side facing you and instep at top, knit across 13 sts on first holder, pick up 14 sts along side edge of instep, knit across 15 instep sts, pick up 14 sts along other side of instep, slip 13 sts from holder to free needle and knit across these sts—69 sts.

Rows 1 through 11:
Knit.

Sole:
Row 1 (right side):
K5, K2 tog; K20, K2 tog; K11, K2 tog; K20, K2 tog; K5—65 sts.

Rows 2, 4, 6, and 8:
Knit.

Row 3:
K4, K2 tog; K20, K2 tog; K9, K2 tog; K20, K2 tog; K4—61 sts.

continued

Blue Skies *(continued)*

Row 5:
K3, K2 tog; K20, K2 tog; K7, K2 tog; K20, K2 tog; K3—
57 sts.

Row 7:
K2, K2 tog; K20, K2 tog; K5, K2 tog; K20, K2 tog; K2—
53 sts.

Row 9:
K1, K2 tog; K20, K2 tog; K3, K2 tog; K20, K2 tog; K1—
49 sts.

Bind off as to knit.

Cut yarn, leaving 8" end for sewing.

Finishing

With tapestry needle, sew bottom and back seam. Cut two 18" lengths of ribbon. Weave ribbon through beading row of each bootie, starting and ending at center front. Tie ends in small bow at center front of each bootie. Trim ends evenly.

Casual Elegance

designed by Sandy Scoville

Experienced knitters only should attempt to create the twists and turns that this pattern takes. For those with the desire, however, this is a very special sweater with rich textural appeal.

Sizing:

Note: Instructions are written for size small; changes for larger sizes are in parentheses.

Size:	Small	Medium	Large
Chest Measurement:	36"-38"	40"-42"	44"-46"
Finished Chest Measurement:	42"	46"	50"

Materials:

Worsted weight yarn, 13 (13, 14) oz [900 (900, 970) yds, 370 (370, 400) g] beige; 8 (8, 9) oz [560 (560, 630) yds, 230 (230, 260) g] each, black, off white, and gray
Size 9 straight or 24" circular knitting needles (your preference), or size required for gauge
Size 7 straight or 24" circular knitting needles (your preference)
Cable needle
Size 16 tapestry needle

Gauge:

With larger size needles, 4½ sts = 1" in stockinette stitch (knit one row, purl one row)

Instructions

Note: When using circular needles, work back and forth in rows.

Back

Note: Color is changed frequently. We recommend carrying the unused colors loosely up the side of your work by bringing the new color under those not in use. This will eliminate the need to weave in so many ends while finishing.

With larger size needles and beige, cast on 94 (106, 112) sts; change to smaller size needles.

Ribbing:

Row 1 (right side):
* K1, P1; rep from * across.

Rep Row 1 in the following color sequence:

☐ beige, 2 rows

☐ gray, 2 rows

- ❏ beige, 2 rows
- ❏ black, 2 rows
- ❏ beige, 2 rows
- ❏ gray, 2 rows
- ❏ beige, 2 rows

Change to larger size needles.

Body:

Row 1:
Continuing with beige, knit.

Row 2:
Purl.

Rows 3 and 4:
With gray, knit.

Rows 5 and 6:
Purl.

Row 7:
With off white, * K2, sl 2 as to purl, K2; rep from
* 14 (16, 17) times more; K2, sl 1 as to purl; K1.

Row 8:
P1, sl 1 as to knit, P2; * P2, sl 2 as to knit, P2; rep from
* 14 (16, 17) times more.

Row 9:
* Sl first 2 sts onto cable needle and hold in back of
work, sl 1 as to purl, K2 from cable needle; sl next st
onto cable needle and hold in front of work, K2,
sl 1 from cable needle as to purl; rep from * 14 (16, 17)
times more; sl next 2 sts onto cable needle and hold in
back of work, sl 1 as to purl, K2 from cable needle; K1.

Row 10:
P3, sl 1 as to knit; * sl 1 as to knit, P4, sl 1 as to knit; rep
from * 14 (16, 17) times more.

Row 11:
With gray, knit.

Row 12:
Purl.

Row 13:
With off white, * sl first st onto cable needle, hold in
front, K2, sl 1 from cable needle as to purl; sl next 2 sts
onto cable needle, hold in back of work, sl 1 as to purl,
K2 from cable needle; rep from * 14 (16, 17) times more;
sl next st onto cable needle, hold in front of work, K2,
sl 1 from cable needle as to purl; K1.

Row 14:
P1, sl l as to knit, P2; * P2, sl 2 as to knit, P2; rep from
* 14 (16, 17) times more.

Row 15:
* K2, sl 2 as to purl, K2; rep from * 14 (16, 17) times
more; K2, sl 1 as to purl; K1.

Row 16:
Rep Row 14.

Rows 17 and 18:
With gray, knit.

Row 19:
Purl.

Row 20:
Purl to last 2 sts; P2 tog.

Row 21:
With beige, knit.

Row 22:
Purl.

Rows 23 and 24:
Rep Rows 21 and 22.

Rows 25 and 26:
With black, knit.

Row 27:
With off white, K2 (3, 1), sl 2 as to purl; * K6, sl 2 as to
purl; rep from * 10 (11, 12) times more; K1 (4, 4).

Row 28:
Purl, slipping the sl sts as to purl.

Rows 29 and 30:
With black, knit.

Row 31:
With beige, knit.

Row 32:
Purl.

Row 33:
Knit.

Row 34:
Purl.

Rows 35 and 36:
With off white, knit.

Row 37:
With black, K2 (7, 5), sl 2 as to purl; * K6, sl 2 as to purl;
rep from * 10 (10, 11) times more; K1 (8, 8).

Row 38:
Purl, slipping the sl sts as to purl.

Rows 39 and 40:
With off white, knit.

continued

Rows 41 through 54:
Rep Rows 21 through 34.

Row 55:
With gray, * K1, yf, sl 1 as to purl, yb; rep from * to last st; K1.

Row 56:
Purl.

Rows 57 through 72:
Rep Rows 55 and 56 in the following color sequence:

❑ black, 2 rows

❑ gray, 2 rows

❑ beige, 2 rows

❑ gray, 2 rows

❑ off white, 2 rows

❑ gray, 2 rows

❑ black, 2 rows

❑ gray, 2 rows

Row 73:
With beige, knit.

Row 74:
Purl.

Row 75:
Knit.

Row 76:
Purl to last st; inc (purl in front and back of st) in last st.

Rep Rows 3 through 72 once.

With beige, continue in stock st (knit one row, purl one row) until back measures 24½" (25", 25") from beg, ending by working a purl row.

Neck Shaping:
Note: Both shoulders are worked at the same time with separate skeins of yarn.

Row 1 (dividing row):
K28 (34, 37); join second skein of beige, bind off center 37 sts; K28 (34, 37).

Row 2:
Purl across both shoulders.

Row 3:
Knit to last 2 sts of first shoulder, K2 tog; on second shoulder, sl 1 as to knit, K1, PSSO; knit across.

Row 4:
Purl.

Bind off all sts.

Front
Work same as back, working 8 rows fewer than back to shoulder bind-off.

Neck Shaping:
Rows 1 through 4:
Rep Rows 1 through 4 of back neck shaping.

Rows 5 through 8:
Rep Rows 3 and 4 of back neck shaping twice.

Bind off all sts.

Sleeve (make 2)
With larger size needles and beige, cast on 42 (46, 50) sts; change to smaller size needles.

Ribbing:
Work in K1, P1 ribbing in same color sequence as for back, inc 10 (12, 14) sts evenly spaced on last row— 52 (58, 64) sts.

Change to larger size needles.

Body:
Row 1:
Knit.

Row 2:
Purl.

Rows 3 and 4:
With gray, knit.

Rows 5 and 6:
Purl.

Row 7:
With off white, * K2, sl 2 as to purl, K2; rep from * to last 4 sts; K2, sl 1 as to purl; K1.

Row 8:
P1, sl 1 as to knit, P2; * P2, sl 2 as to knit, P2; rep from * 7 (8, 9) times more.

Row 9:
* Sl next 2 sts onto cable needle and hold in back, sl 1 as to purl, K2 from cable needle; sl next st onto cable needle and hold in front, K2, sl 1 from cable needle as to purl; rep from * 7 (8, 9) times more; sl next 2 sts onto cable needle and hold in back, sl 1 as to purl, K2 from cable needle; K1.

Row 10:
P3, sl 1 as to knit; * sl 1 as to knit, P4, sl 1 as to knit; rep from * 7 (8, 9) times more.

Row 11:
With gray, knit.

Row 12:
Purl.

Row 13:
With off white, * sl first st onto cable needle, hold in front, K2, sl 1 from cable needle as to purl; sl next 2 sts onto cable needle, hold in back, sl 1 as to purl, K2 from cable needle; rep from * 7 (8, 9) times more; sl next st onto cable needle, hold in front, K2, sl 1 from cable needle as to purl; K1.

Row 14:
P1, sl 1 as to knit, P2; * P2, sl 2 as to knit, P2; rep from * 7 (8, 9) times more.

Row 15:
* K2, sl 2 as to purl, K2; rep from * 7 (8, 9) times more; K2, sl 1 as to purl; K1.

Row 16:
P1, sl 1 as to knit, P2; * P2, sl 2 as to knit, P2; rep from * 7 (8, 9) times more.

Rows 17 and 18:
With gray, knit.

Rows 19 and 20:
Purl.

Row 21:
With beige, K1, inc; knit to last 2 sts; inc; K1—54 (60, 66) sts.

Row 22:
Purl.

Row 23:
Knit.

Row 24:
Purl.

Row 25:
With black, K1, inc; knit to last 2 sts; inc; K1—56 (62, 68) sts.

Row 26:
Knit.

Row 27:
With off white, K2 (2, 4), sl 2 as to purl; * K6, sl 2; rep from * 5 (6, 6) times more; K4 (2, 6).

Row 28:
Purl, slipping the sl sts as to purl.

Row 29:
With black, K1, inc; knit to last 2 sts; inc; K1—58 (64, 70) sts.

Row 30:
Knit.

Row 31:
With beige, knit.

Row 32:
Purl.

Row 33:
K1, inc; knit to last 2 sts; inc; K1—60 (66, 72) sts.

Row 34:
Purl.

Rows 35 and 36:
With off white, knit.

Row 37:
With black, K6 (6, 2), sl 2 as to purl; * K6, sl 2 as to purl; rep from * 5 (6, 7) times more; K4 (2, 4).

Row 38:
Purl, slipping the sl sts as to purl.

Row 39:
With off white, K1, inc; knit to last 2 sts; inc; K1—62 (68, 74) sts.

Row 40:
Knit.

Rows 41 through 46:
Rep Rows 21 through 26. At end of Row 46—66 (72, 78) sts.

Row 47:
With off white, K4 (4, 2), sl 2 as to knit; * K6, sl 2 as to knit; rep from * across, ending K4 (2, 2).

Rows 48 through 54:
Rep Rows 28 through 34, inc 1 st at end of Row 54. At end of Row 54—71 (77, 83) sts.

Row 55:
With gray, * K1, yf, sl 1 as to purl, yb; rep from * to last st; K1.

Row 56:
Purl.

Rows 57 through 72:
Rep Rows 55 and 56 in the same color sequence as for back, inc 1 st at each end of Rows 61, 65, and 69, and adjusting patt to accomodate increases. At end of Row 72—77 (83, 89) sts.

Row 73:
With beige, knit.

Row 74:
Purl.

continued

Row 75:
Knit.

Row 76:
Purl across to last 2 sts; inc; P1—78 **(84, 90)** sts.

Rep patt beg with Row 3 of sleeve and ending with Row 54, eliminating all increases.

With beige, continue in stock st **(knit one row, purl one row)** until sleeve measures 19" **(20", 21")**.

Bind off loosely.

Neckline Ribbing:
Sew left shoulder seam.

Starting at right shoulder with smaller size needle and beige, pick up 2 sts along back neckline edge, 37 sts across back edge, 2 sts along left back neckline edge, 8 sts along left front edge, 37 sts across front edge, and 8 sts along right front edge—94 sts.

Row 1:
* K1, P1; rep from * across.

Rep Row 1 until ribbing measures 1½" from picked up sts.

Bind off loosely in ribbing.

Finishing
Step 1:
Sew right shoulder and neckline seam.

Step 2:
Holding right sides together, match center of last rows of sleeves to shoulder seams. Sew sleeves to body.

Step 3:
Sew side and sleeve seams, matching stripes.

Weave in all ends.

Country Weekend for Her
designed by Kathy Wesley

Relax and enjoy a sweater that is as easy to knit as it is easy to wear. This flattering tunic style pairs up well with jeans, slacks or longer skirts.

Sizing:
Note: Instructions are written for size small; changes for larger sizes are in parentheses.

Size:	Small	Medium	Large
Chest Measurement:	34"-36"	38"-40"	42"-44"
Finished Chest Measurement:	46"	50"	54"

Materials:
Worsted weight brushed yarn, dk blue ombre, 12 **(14, 16)** oz, **[**1080 **(**1260, 1440**)** yds, 360 **(**420, 480**)** g**]**
Size 7, 24" circular knitting needle, or size required for gauge
Size 15, 24" circular knitting needle
Size 7, 16" circular knitting needle **(for collar)**
Two 6¼" stitch holders
Two 4" stitch holders
Size 16 tapestry needle

Gauge:
With smaller size needle, 5 sts = 1" in stockinette stitch **(knit one row, purl one row)**
6 rows = 1"

Instructions
Note: Purl side is right side of garment.

Back
With smaller size needle, loosely cast on 70 **(76, 82)** sts.

Row 1 (right side):
With larger size needle, purl.

Row 2:
With smaller size needle, knit.

Rep Rows 1 and 2 until piece measures 27" **(28", 29")**, ending by working a wrong side row.

Next Row:
Rep Row 1.

Shoulder Shaping:
Row 1:
With smaller size needle, loosely bind off 10 **(11, 12)** sts, knit across.

Row 2:
With larger size needle, bind off 10 (11, 12) sts, purl across.

Row 3:
With smaller size needle, loosely bind off 11 (11, 12) sts, knit across.

Row 4:
With larger size needle, bind off 11 (11, 12) sts, place rem 28 (32, 34) sts onto a stitch holder for neckline.

Front
Work the same as back until piece measures 25" (26", 27") or 2" less than back to shoulder shaping, ending by working a purl row.

Neck Shaping:
Row 1:
Knit first 31 (33, 35) sts for first shoulder, slip next 8 (10, 12) sts onto a stitch holder for neck; join second skein of yarn, knit rem 31 (33, 35) sts for second shoulder.

Row 2:
Purl across sts on second shoulder; bind off 5 (5, 5) sts on first shoulder for neck, purl across.

Row 3:
Knit across first shoulder; loosely bind off 5 (5, 5) sts on second shoulder for neck; knit across.

Row 4:
Purl across second shoulder; bind off 5 (6, 6) sts on first shoulder for neck; purl across.

Row 5:
Knit across first shoulder; loosely bind off first 5 (6, 6) sts on second shoulder for neck, knit across— 21 (22, 25) sts on each shoulder.

Continuing to work across both shoulders, work even until piece measures same as back to shoulder shaping, ending by working a purl row.

Shoulder Shaping:
Row 1:
Loosely bind off 10 (11, 12) sts; knit across.

Row 2:
Bind off 10 (11, 12) sts; purl across.

Row 3:
Loosely bind off 11 (11, 12) sts; knit across.

Bind off rem sts.

Sleeve (make 2)
With smaller size needles, cast on 32 (37, 42) sts.

Cuff:
Row 1 (right side):
Knit.

Rows 2 through 7:
Rep Row 1.

Row 8:
* K2 tog; K3; rep from * 5 (6, 7) times more; K2 tog— 25 (29, 33) sts.

Body:
Row 1 (right side):
With larger size needle, purl.

Row 2:
With smaller size needle, knit.

Row 3:
Rep Row 1.

Row 4:
With smaller size needle, K1, inc (knit in front and back of next st); knit to last 2 sts; inc; K1.

Rep Rows 1 through 4, 17 (18, 19) times—59 (65, 70) sts.

continued

Country Weekend for Her (continued)

Rep Rows 1 and 2 until piece measures 17½" (18", 18½").

Bind off all stitches.

Sew shoulder seams.

Collar

Hold sweater with right side facing you and neckline at top.

With 16"-circular needle, K28 (32, 34) sts from back neck-line holder, pick up 12 (14, 16) sts along left neck edge, K8 (10, 12) sts from front neckline holder, pick up 12 (14, 16) sts along right neck edge—60 (70, 78) sts.

Note: Mark beg of rnds.

Rnd 1:
Knit.

Rnds 2 through 14:
Rep Rnd 1.

With larger size needle, bind off all sts.

Collar will roll naturally to right side of sweater.

Finishing
Step 1:
Mark 10" (11", 11½") from shoulder seam on both edges of front and back. Match center of sleeves to shoulder seams and edge of sleeves to marked stitch on front and back. Sew in place.

Step 2:
Sew side and sleeve seams.

Country Weekend for Kids

designed by Kathy Wesley

This speedy-knit unisex design works up so fast you won't have to worry that they might outgrow it before you're done.

Sizing:
Note: Instructions are written for size small; changes for larger sizes are in parentheses.

Size:	Small (4-6)	Medium (8-10)	Large (12-14)
Finished Chest Measurement:	28"	32"	36"

Materials:
Worsted weight brushed yarn, lt blue ombre, 6 (8, 10) oz, [540 (720, 900) yds, 180 (240, 300) g]
Size 7, 24" circular knitting needle, or size required for gauge
Size 15, 24" circular knitting needle
Size 7, 16" circular knitting needle (for collar)
Two 4" stitch holders
Size 16 tapestry needle

Gauge:
With smaller size needle,
5 sts = 1" in stockinette stitch (knit one row, purl one row)
6 rows = 1"

Instructions

Back

Ribbing:
With smaller size needle, loosely cast on 63 (71, 81) sts.

Row 1 (right side):
K1; * P1, K1; rep from * across.

Row 2:
P1; * K1, P1; rep from * across.

Rep Rows 1 and 2 until piece measures 1½" (1½", 2"), ending by working a Row 2.

Next Row:
Rep Row 1.

Next Row:
K0 (1, 0); * K2 tog; K1; rep from * 20 (22, 26) times more; K0 (1, 0)—42 (48, 54) sts.

Body:
Row 1 (right side):
With larger size needle, purl.

Row 2:
With smaller size needle, knit.

Rep Rows 1 and 2 until piece measures 16" (18", 20"), ending by working a Row 2.

Next Row:
Rep Row 1.

Shoulder Shaping:
Row 1 (wrong side):
With smaller size needle, loosely bind off 6 (7, 8) sts; knit across.

Row 2 (right side):
With larger size needle, bind off 6 (7, 8) sts; purl across.

Row 3:
With smaller size needle, loosely bind off 6 (6, 7) sts; knit across.

Row 4:
With larger size needle, bind off 6 (6, 7) sts; place rem 18 (22, 24) sts onto a stitch holder for neckline.

Front
Work the same as back until piece measures 14" (16", 18") or 2" less than back to shoulder shaping, ending by working a purl row.

Neckline Shaping:
Row 1 (wrong side):
With smaller size needle, for first shoulder, K18 (20, 22); slip next 6 (8, 10) sts onto a stitch holder for neckline; for second shoulder, join second skein of yarn, K18 (20, 22).

Row 2 (right side):
With larger size needle, for second shoulder, purl across; for first shoulder, bind off 3 (3, 3) sts; purl across.

Row 3:
With smaller size needle, for first shoulder, knit across; for second shoulder, loosely bind off 3 (3, 3) sts; knit across.

Row 4:
With larger size needle, for second shoulder, purl across; for first shoulder, bind off 3 (4, 4) sts; purl across.

Row 5:
With smaller size needle, for first shoulder, knit across; for second shoulder, loosely bind off 3 (4, 4) sts; knit across—12 (13, 15) sts on each shoulder.

Continuing to work across both shoulders, work even until piece measures same as back to shoulder shaping, ending by working a purl row.

Shoulder Shaping:
Row 1:
With smaller size needle, loosely bind off 6 (7, 8) sts; knit across.

Row 2:
With larger size needle, bind off 6 (7, 8) sts; purl across.

Row 3:
With smaller size needle, loosely bind off 6 (6, 7) sts; knit across.

Row 4:
With larger size needle, bind off rem sts.

Sleeve (make 2)
Ribbing:
With smaller size needle, cast on 25 (27, 29) sts.

Row 1 (right side):
K1; * P1, K1; rep from * across.

Row 2:
P1; * K1, P1; rep from * across.

Rep Rows 1 and 2 until piece measures 1½", ending by working a Row 2.

Next Row:
Rep Row 1.

Next Row:
K2 (3, 5); * K2 tog; K1; rep from * 6 times more; K2 (3, 3)—18 (20, 22) sts.

Body:
Row 1 (right side):
With larger size needle, purl.

Row 2:
With smaller size needle, knit.

Row 3:
Rep Row 1.

Row 4:
With smaller size needle, K1, inc (knit in front and back of next st); knit to last 3 sts; inc; K1.

continued

Rep Rows 1 through 4 until there are 40 (46, 52) sts on needle.

Rep Rows 1 and 2 until piece measures 11" (13", 15"), ending by working a Row 2.

Bind off all sts.

Sew shoulder seams.

Collar

Hold sweater with right side facing you and neckline at top.

With 16" circular needle, K18 (22, 24) sts from back neckline holder, pick up 16 (18, 20) sts along left neck edge, K6 (8, 10) sts from front neckline holder, pick up 16 (18, 20) sts along right neck edge—56 (66, 74) sts.

Note: Mark beg of rnds.

Rnd 1:
Knit.

Rnds 2 through 12:
Rep Rnd 1.

With larger size needle, bind off all sts.

Collar will roll naturally to right side of sweater.

Finishing
Step 1:
Mark 6½" (7½", 8½") from shoulder seam on both edges of front and back. Match center of sleeves to shoulder seams and edge of sleeves to marked stitches on front and back. Sew in place.

Step 2:
Sew side and sleeve seams. Weave in all ends.

Country Weekend for Teddy

designed by Kathy Wesley

Kids (and adults, too) will love having a sweater for Teddy in the same relaxed style as their own sweater.

Size:
Fits 12" craft bear
Finished Chest Measurement: 14"

Materials:
Worsted weight brushed yarn, 3 oz (270 yds, 90 g) lt blue ombre
Size 7, straight knitting needles, or size required for gauge
Size 15 straight knitting needles
Two 4" stitch holders
Size 16 tapestry needle

Gauge:
With smaller size needles, 5 sts = 1" in stockinette stitch (knit one row, purl one row)
6 rows = 1"

Instructions
Back/Front (make 2)
Ribbing:
With smaller size needles, loosely cast on 31 sts.

Row 1 (right side):
K1; * P1, K1; rep from * across.

Row 2:
P1; * K1, P1; rep from * across.

Row 3:
Rep Row 1.

Body:
Note: Body is worked with one large size needle and one small size needle.

Row 1 (wrong side):
With smaller size needle, K1; * K2 tog; K1; rep from * across—21 sts.

Row 2 (right side):
With larger size needle, purl.

Row 3 (wrong side):
With smaller needle, knit.

Repeat Rows 2 and 3 until piece measures 4", ending by working a Row 3.

Place sts onto a stitch holder for neck.

Sleeve (make 2)

Ribbing:
With smaller size needles, cast on 25 sts.

Row 1 (right side):
K1; * P1, K1; rep from * across.

Row 2:
P1; * K1, P1; rep from * across.

Row 3:
Rep Row 1.

Body:
Row 1 (wrong side):
With smaller size needle, knit.

Row 2 (right side):
With larger size needle, purl.

Repeat Rows 1 and 2 until piece measures 2", ending by working a Row 2.

Next Row:
Rep Row 1.

With larger size needle, bind off as to purl.

Collar
Row 1:
Hold back with right side facing you; with smaller size needles, K21 sts from back stitch holder, K21 sts from front stitch holder—42 sts.

Row 2:
Purl.

Row 3:
Knit.

Rows 4 through 7:
Rep Rows 2 and 3 twice more.

Row 8:
Rep Row 2.

With larger size needle, bind off as to knit.

Collar will roll naturally to right side of sweater.

Finishing
Step 1:
With tapestry needle and yarn, sew collar seam.

Step 2:
Matching center of sleeves to shoulder seams and edge of sleeves to first row of body above ribbing, sew sleeves in place. Sew side ribbing and sleeve seams. Weave in all ends.

Feminine Touch

Whether worn with a tailored suit or a soft, flowing skirt, this versatile lacy sweater is the perfect accompaniment. The challenging pattern stitch used makes it an ideal project for experienced knitters.

Sizing:
Note: Instructions are written for size small; changes for larger sizes are in parentheses.

Size:	Small	Medium	Large
Chest Measurement:	30"-32"	34"-36"	38"-40"
Finished Chest Measurement:	38"	42"	46"

Materials:
Sport weight yarn with a cotton look such as Luster Sheen®, 14 (16, 18) oz [1260 (1440, 1530) yds, 397 (475, 551) g] off white
Size 6 straight knitting needles, or size required for gauge
Markers
Two 6¼" stitch holders
Size 16 tapestry needle

Gauge:
6 sts = 1" in stockinette stitch (knit one row, purl one row)
8 rows = 1"

Instructions

Back
Cast on 121 (131, 141) sts.

Ribbing:
Row 1 (right side):
K1; * P1, K1; rep from * across.

Row 2:
P1; * K1, P1; rep from * across.

Rows 3 through 6:
Rep Rows 1 and 2 twice more.

Row 7:
Rep Row 1.

Row 8:
P1, inc (knit in front and back of next st); P1; * K1, P1; rep from * across—122 (132, 142) sts.

Body:
Row 1 (right side):
K5; * YO, K1, K2 tog tbl; K7; rep from * 10 (11, 12) times more; YO, K1, K2 tog tbl; K4.

continued

Row 2:
P3; * P2 tog tbl; P1, YO, P7; rep from * 10 (11, 12) times more; P2 tog tbl; P1, YO, P6.

Row 3:
K7; * YO, K1, K2 tog tbl; K7; rep from * 10 (11, 12) times more; YO, K1, K2 tog tbl; K2.

Row 4:
P1; * P2 tog tbl; P1, YO, P7; rep from * 10 (11, 12) times more; P2 tog tbl; P1, YO, P8.

Row 5:
K4; * YO, K1, K2 tog tbl; K7; rep from * 10 (11, 12) times more; YO, K1, K2 tog tbl; K5.

Row 6:
P6; * P2 tog tbl; P1, YO, P7; rep from * 10 (11, 12) times more; P2 tog tbl; P1, YO, P3.

Row 7:
K2; * YO, K1, K2 tog tbl; K7; rep from * 10 (11, 12) times more; YO, K1, K2 tog tbl; K7.

Row 8:
P8; * P2 tog tbl; P1, YO, P7; rep from * 10 (11, 12) times more; P2 tog tbl; P1, YO, P1.

Rep Rows 1 through 8 until piece measures 14" (15", 15"). Mark beg and end of last row for underarm.

Continue to rep Rows 1 through 8 until back measures 6" (7", 8") above marker, ending on a wrong side row.

Neck and Shoulder Shaping:
Note: Both shoulders are worked at the same time with separate skeins of yarn.

Row 1 (dividing row):
Continuing in patt as established, work across first 42 (46, 50) sts for right shoulder; drop yarn; slip next 38 (40, 42) sts onto a stitch holder for neck; join another skein of yarn; work across rem 42 (46, 50) sts for left shoulder.

Row 2:
In patt, work across left shoulder to last 2 sts; P2 tog; on right shoulder, sl 1 as to purl, P1, PSSO; continue in patt across.

Row 3:
In patt, work across right shoulder to last 2 sts; K2 tog; on left shoulder, sl 1 as to knit, K1, PSSO; continue in patt across.

Rows 4 through 7:
Rep Rows 2 and 3 twice more.

Row 8:
Rep Row 2.

Row 9:
Bind off 20 (22, 24) sts; work in patt to last 2 sts; K2 tog; on left shoulder, sl 1 as to knit, K1, PSSO; work in patt across.

Row 10:
Bind off 20 (22, 24) sts; work in patt to last 2 sts; P2 tog; on right shoulder, sl 1 as to purl, P1, PSSO; work in patt across.

Row 11:
Bind off 7 (8, 9) sts; work in patt to last 2 sts; K2 tog; on left shoulder, sl 1 as to knit, K1, PSSO; work in patt across.

Row 12:
Bind off 7 (8, 9) sts; work in patt to last 2 sts; P2 tog; on right shoulder, sl 1 as to purl, P1, PSSO; work in patt across.

Row 13:
Bind off to last 2 sts; K2 tog; bind off; on left shoulder, sl 1, K1, PSSO, bind off rem sts.

Front
Work same as back until piece measures 8 rows less than back to neck and shoulder shaping.

Neck and Shoulder Shaping:
Row 1 (dividing row):
Continuing in patt as established, work across first 50 (54, 58) sts for left shoulder; drop yarn; slip next 22 (24, 26) sts onto a stitch holder for neck; join another skein of yarn; work in patt across rem sts for right shoulder.

Row 2:
In patt, work across right shoulder to last 2 sts; P2 tog; on left shoulder, sl 1 as to purl, P1, PSSO; continue in patt across.

Row 3:
In patt, work across left shoulder to last 2 sts; K2 tog; on right shoulder, sl 1 as to knit, K1, PSSO; continue in patt across.

Rows 4 through 15:
Rep Rows 2 and 3 six times more.

Row 16:
Rep Row 2.

Row 17:
Bind off 20 (22, 24) sts; work in patt to last 2 sts; K2 tog; on right shoulder, sl 1 as to knit, K1, PSSO; work in patt across.

Row 18:
Bind off 20 **(22, 24)** sts; work in patt to last 2 sts; P2 tog; on left shoulder, sl 1 as to purl, P1, PSSO; work in patt across.

Row 19:
Bind off 7 **(8, 9)** sts; work in patt to last 2 sts; K2 tog; on right shoulder, sl 1 as to knit, K1, PSSO; work in patt across.

Row 20:
Bind off 7 **(8, 9)** sts; work in patt to last 2 sts; P2 tog; on left shoulder, sl 1 as to purl, P1, PSSO; work in patt across.

Row 21:
Bind off to last 2 sts; K2 tog; bind off; on right shoulder, sl 1 as to knit, K1, PSSO; bind off rem sts.

Sleeve (make 2)
Cast on 75 **(79, 83)** sts.

Ribbing:
Rows 1 through 7:
Rep Rows 1 through 7 of Back ribbing.

Row 8 (increase row):

Small Size Only:
P1, (inc, P1) 8 times; * K1, P1, inc; P1; rep from * 9 times more; (inc, P1) 9 times—102 sts.

Medium Size Only:
P1, (inc, P1) 15 times; * K1, P1, inc; P1; rep from * 5 times more; (inc, P1) 12 times—112 sts.

Large Size Only:
P1, (inc, P1) 8 times; * K1, P1, inc; P1; rep from * 11 times more; (inc, P1) 9 times—112 sts.

Body:
Row 1 (right side):
K5; * YO, K1, K2 tog tbl; K7; rep from * 8 **(9, 9)** times more; YO, K1, K2 tog tbl; K4.

Row 2:
P3; * P2 tog tbl; P1, YO, P7; rep from * 8 **(9, 9)** times more; P2 tog tbl; P1, YO, P6.

Row 3:
K7; * YO, K1, K2 tog tbl; K7; rep from * 8 **(9, 9)** times more; YO, K1, K2 tog tbl; K2.

Row 4:
P1; * P2 tog tbl; P1, YO, P7; rep from * 8 **(9, 9)** times more; P2 tog tbl; P1, YO, P8.

Row 5:
K4; * YO, K1, K2 tog tbl; K7; rep from * 8 **(9, 9)** times more; YO, K1, K2 tog tbl; K5.

Row 6:
P6; * P2 tog tbl; P1, YO, P7; rep from * 8 **(9, 9)** times more; P2 tog tbl; P3.

Row 7:
K2; * YO, K1, K2 tog tbl; K7; rep from * 8 **(9, 9)** times more; YO, K1, K2 tog tbl; K7.

Row 8:
P8; * P2 tog tbl; P1, YO, P7; rep from * 8 **(9, 9)** times more; P2 tog tbl; P1.

Rep Rows 1 through 8 until sleeve measures 7" **(8", 8")**.

Bind off all sts.

Sew right shoulder seam.

Neck Ribbing:
Row 1:
With right side facing you, join yarn at left shoulder seam, pick up 20 sts along left front neck shaping, slip 22 **(22, 24)** sts from stitch holder to free needle and knit across these sts; pick up 20 sts along right front neck shaping to shoulder seam; pick up 13 sts along right back neck shaping, slip 38 **(40, 42)** sts from stitch holder to free needle and knit across these sts; pick up 13 sts along left back neck shaping—126 **(128, 132)** sts.

Row 2:
* K1, P1; rep from * across.

Rows 3 through 8:
Rep Row 1.

Bind off in ribbing.

Finishing
Step 1:
Sew left shoulder and neck ribbing seam.

Step 2:
Sew sleeves to body between markers, matching center of sleeves to shoulder seams.

Step 3:
Sew sleeve and side seams. Weave in all ends.

Flirty Scarf

Wear this quick-to-knit scarf fashioned with eyelash-type yarn and you're sure to turn an eye or two. This versatile accessory will flatter women of all ages.

Size:
About 10" x 42"

Materials:
"Eyelash" type synethic fingering or sport weight yarn, 1½ oz (170 yds, 40 g) in color of your choice
Size 13 straight knitting needles, or size required for gauge
Size 16 tapestry needle

Gauge:
3 sts = about 1" in garter stitch (knit every row)

Instructions
Loosely cast on 32 sts, leaving a 12" end at beg.

Row 1:
Knit.

Rep Row 1 until scarf measures 42" long, or until about 3 yds of yarn remain.

Bind off loosely, leaving a 12" end.

Weave in ends along each edge.

Gloves for Her

This classic glove is a great project for using tweedy yarns in a shade to set off your look on a wintry day.

Size:
Glove sizes 6—7

Materials:
Worsted weight yarn, 3 oz (210 yds, 90 g) purple tweed
Size 6, 7" double-pointed knitting needles, or size required for gauge
6 safety pins (for stitch holders)
Size 18 tapestry needle

Gauge:
5 sts = 1" in stockinette stitch (knit one row, purl one row)
7 rows = 1"

Instructions

Right Glove
Cast on 36 sts; divide by placing first 12 sts on one needle, 12 sts on second needle, and 12 sts on third needle; join, being careful not to twist sts (see Special Techniques on page 6).

Note: Mark first st with contrasting color for beg of rnds.

Ribbing:
Rnd 1:
∗ K2, P2; rep from ∗ around.

Rep Rnd 1 until piece measures 3".

Palm:
Rnds 1 through 3:
Knit.

Thumb Gusset:
Rnd 1:
Knit to last 2 sts on third needle; inc (knit in front and back of next st); K1—37 sts.

Rnds 2 and 3:
Knit.

Rnd 4:
Knit to last 3 sts on third needle; inc in each of next 2 sts; K1—39 sts.

Rnds 5 and 6:
Knit.

Rnd 7:
Knit to last 5 sts on third needle; inc; K2, inc; K1—41 sts.

Rnds 8 and 9:
Knit.

Rnd 10:
Knit to last 7 sts on third needle; inc; K4, inc; K1—43 sts.

Rnds 11 and 12:
Knit.

Rnd 13:
Knit to last 9 sts on third needle; inc; K6, inc; K1—45 sts.

Rnds 14 and 15:
Knit.

Dividing Rnd for Thumb:
K34; slip rem 11 sts to holder for thumb; cast on 2 sts (see **Figs 1** and **2**); continuing in rnds, knit even until palm measures 1½" above thumb sts, or desired length, to beg of fingers— 36 sts.

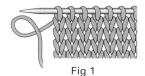

Fig 1

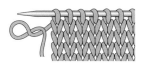

Fig 2

Dividing Rnd for Fingers:
K2, cast on 2 sts; leave these 4 sts on needle for part of index finger; slip next 5 sts onto a holder for one side of middle finger; slip next 4 sts onto a holder for part of ring finger; slip next 8 sts onto a holder for little finger; slip next 4 sts onto a holder for other side of ring finger; slip next 5 sts onto a holder for other side of middle finger; slip next 4 sts onto second needle for part of index finger; slip last 4 sts on third needle for part of index finger.

Index Finger:
Join and knit on 12 sts in rnds until finger measures 2½", or desired length.

Decrease Rnd:
(K2 tog) 6 times—6 sts.

Cut yarn, leaving a 6" end. Thread end into tapestry needle and weave through sts. Draw up tightly and weave in end securely.

Middle Finger:
Slip sts from holders (one on each side of index finger) onto 2 needles. With free needle, pick up 1 st in each cast-on st at base of index finger; with free needle, K5, cast on 1 st; with rem free needle, K5. Divide these 13 sts, placing 4 sts on one needle, 4 sts on second needle, and 5 sts on third needle; knit even in rnds until finger measures 2¾", or desired length.

Decrease Rnd:
(K2 tog) 6 times; K1—7 sts.

Cut yarn, leaving a 6" end. Thread end into tapestry

needle and weave through sts. Draw up tightly and weave in end securely.

Ring Finger:
Slip sts from holders (one on each side of middle finger) to 2 needles. With free needle, pick up 2 sts in cast-on st at base of middle finger; with free needle, K4, cast on 1 st; with rem free needle, K4; divide these 11 sts, placing 4 sts on one needle, 4 sts on second needle, and 3 sts on third needle; knit even in rnds until finger measures 2½", or desired length.

Decrease Rnd:
(K2 tog) 5 times; K1— 6 sts.

Cut yarn, leaving a 6" end. Thread end into tapestry needle and weave through sts. Draw up tightly and weave in end securely.

Little Finger:
Slip 4 sts from holder to one needle and 4 sts from same holder to second needle. With third needle, pick up 2 sts in cast-on st at base of ring finger; knit in rnds until finger measures 2¼", or desired length.

Decrease Rnd:
(K2 tog) 5 times—5 sts.

Cut yarn, leaving a 6" end. Thread end into tapestry needle and weave through sts. Draw up tightly and weave in end securely.

Thumb:
Slip 11 sts from holder to free needle; with a second free needle, pick up 3 sts in cast-on sts. Divide these 14 sts, placing 4 sts on one needle, 4 sts on second needle, and 6 sts on third needle; knit even in rnds until thumb measures 2¼", or desired length.

Decrease Rnd:
(K2 tog) 7 times—7 sts.

Cut yarn, leaving a 6" end. Thread end into tapestry needle and weave through sts. Draw up tightly and weave in end securely.

continued

Gloves for Her *(continued)*

Left Glove

Work same as for Right Glove to Dividing Rnd For Fingers.

Dividing Rnd For Fingers:

K8, cast on 2 sts and leave these 10 sts on needle for part of index finger; slip next 5 sts onto holder for one side of middle finger; slip next 4 sts onto holder for one side of ring finger; slip next 8 sts onto holder for little finger; slip next 4 sts onto holder for other side of ring finger; slip next 5 sts onto holder for other side of middle finger; leave last 2 sts on needle for rem part of index finger. Now divide sts for index finger onto 3 needles as follows: 4 sts on first needle, 4 sts on second needle, and 4 sts on third needle.

Work fingers and thumb same as for Right Glove.

Weave in all ends.

Handsome Fisherman

designed by Sandy Scoville

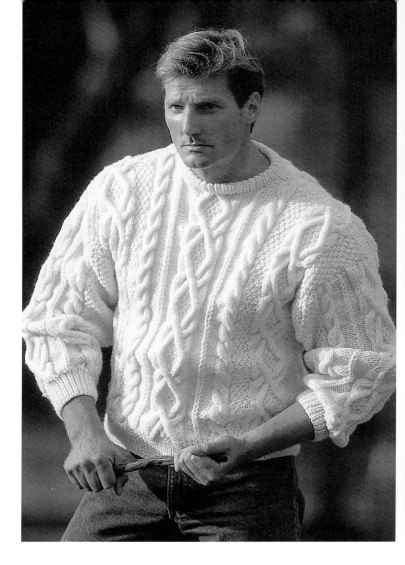

Experienced knitters will savor the beautiful, traditional stitches that have been adapted from sweaters worn by fishermen in the Aran Islands off the coast of Ireland.

Sizing:

Note: Instructions are written for size small; changes for larger sizes are in parentheses.

Size:	Small	Medium	Large
Chest Measurement:	36"-38"	40"-42"	44"-46"
Finished Chest Measurement:	42"	46"	50"

Materials:

Worsted weight yarn, 40 (42, 44) oz [1600 (1700, 1800) yds, 1143 (1200, 1257) g] off white

Size 9 straight or 24" circular knitting needles (your preference), or size required for gauge

Size 7 straight or 24" circular knitting needles (your preference)

Size 7, 16" circular knitting needle (for neck)

Markers

Cable needle

Size 16 tapestry needle

Gauge:

With larger size needles, 4 sts = 1" in seed stitch
With larger size needles, 6 sts = 1¼" in cable patt

Pattern Stitches

Seed Stitch:
Row 1 (foundation row):
* P1, K1; rep from * across.

Row 2:
Knit the knit sts, purl the purl sts.

Row 3:
Knit the purl sts, purl the knit sts.

Row 4:
Knit the knit sts, purl the purl sts.

Rep Rows 3 and 4 for patt.

Double Cable (worked over 18 sts):
Row 1 (right side):
K1; slip next 3 sts onto cable needle, hold in front of work, K1, K3 from cable needle; (P1, K1) 4 times; slip next st onto cable needle, hold in back of work, K3, K1 from cable needle; K1.

Row 2 and all even numbered rows:
Knit the knit sts, purl the purl sts.

32

Row 3:
K2, slip next 3 sts onto cable needle, hold in front of work, K1, K3 from cable needle; (P1, K1) 3 times; slip next st onto cable needle, hold in back of work, K3, K1 from cable needle; K2.

Row 5:
K3, slip next 3 sts onto cable needle, hold in front of work, K1, K3 from cable needle; (P1, K1) twice; slip next st onto cable needle, hold in back of work, K3, K1 from cable needle; K3.

Row 7:
K4, slip next 3 sts onto cable needle, hold in front of work, K1, K3 from cable needle; P1, K1; slip next st onto cable needle, hold in back of work, K3, K1 from cable needle; K4.

Row 9:
K5, slip next 3 sts onto cable needle, hold in front of work, K1, K3 from cable needle; slip next st onto cable needle, hold in back of work, K3, K1 from cable needle; K5.

Row 11:
† Slip next 3 sts onto cable needle, hold in back of work, K3, K3 from cable needle †; slip next 3 sts onto cable needle, hold in front of work, K3, K3 from cable needle; rep from † to † once.

Row 13:
K5, slip next st onto cable needle, hold in back of work, K3, K1 from cable needle; slip next 3 sts onto cable needle, hold in front of work, K1, K3 from cable needle; K5.

Row 15:
K4, slip next st onto cable needle, hold in back of work, K3, K1 from cable needle; K1, P1; slip next 3 sts onto cable needle, hold in front of work, K1, K3 from cable needle; K4.

Row 17:
K3, slip next st onto cable needle, hold in back of work, K3, K1 from cable needle; (K1, P1) twice; slip next 3 sts onto cable needle, hold in front of work, K1, K3 from cable needle; K3.

Row 19:
K2, slip next st onto cable needle, hold in back of work, K3, K1 from cable needle; (K1, P1) 3 times; slip next 3 sts onto cable needle, hold in front of work, K1, K3 from cable needle; K2.

Row 21:
K1, slip next st onto cable needle, hold in back of work, K3, K1 from cable needle; (K1, P1) 4 times; slip next 3 sts onto cable needle, hold in front of work, K1, K3 from cable needle; K1.

Rep Rows 1 through 22 for patt.

Cable Front (CF):
(worked over 6 sts)

Row 1:
Knit.

Row 2:
Purl.

Rows 3 and 4:
Rep Rows 1 and 2.

Row 5:
Slip next 3 sts onto cable needle, hold in front of work, K3, K3 from cable needle.

Row 6:
Purl.

Rows 7 and 8:
Rep Rows 1 and 2.

Cable Back (CB):
(worked over 6 sts)

Row 1:
Knit.

Row 2:
Purl.

Rows 3 and 4:
Rep Rows 1 and 2.

Row 5:
Slip next 3 sts onto cable needle, hold in back of work, K3, K3 from cable needle.

Row 6:
Purl.

Rows 7 and 8:
Rep Rows 1 and 2.

Instructions
Note: Markers are used to separate pattern stitches. They are set in place on the foundation row, and should be moved from the left-hand needle to the right-hand needle as you come to them. They may be removed when you are familiar with the pattern.
When using circular needles, work back and forth in rows.

Back
Ribbing:
With larger size needles, cast on 108 (116, 124) sts; change to smaller size needles.

Row 1:
* K1, P1; rep from * across.

continued

Rep Row 1 until back measures 3". Change to larger size needles.

Note: When working foundation row, refer to Pattern Stitches on pages 32 and 33.

Body:
Row 1 (foundation row):
(P1, K1) 2 (3, 5) times—Seed St; place marker; Double Cable patt over next 18 sts; place marker; (P1, K1) 2 (3, 3) times—Seed St; place marker; P2; CF; place marker; P5, K1 in st below, P5, place marker; Double Cable patt over next 18 sts; place marker; P5, K1 in st below, P5; place marker; CB; place marker; P2; (P1, K1) 2 (3, 3) times—Seed St; place marker; Double Cable patt over next 18 sts; place marker; (P1, K1) 2 (3, 5) times—Seed St.

Row 2:
Keeping to patt on Seed St, knit all other knit sts and purl all other purl sts.

Referring to Pattern Stitches on pages 32 and 33, continue in patt until back measures 24½" (25", 25").

Neck Shaping:
Note: Both shoulders are worked at the same time with separate skeins of yarn.

Row 1 (dividing row):
Work in patt across 39 (43, 47) sts for first shoulder; join second skein of yarn; bind off center 30 sts; work in patt across second shoulder.

Row 2:
Work in patt across both shoulders.

Row 3:
Work in patt to last 2 sts of first shoulder; P2 tog; on second shoulder, sl 1, P1, PSSO, work in patt across.

Row 4:
Rep Row 2.

Bind off all sts.

Front
Work same as for back, working 6 rows less than back to neck shaping.

Neck Shaping:
Rows 1 through 4:
Rep Rows 1 through 4 of back neck shaping.

Rows 5 and 6:
Rep Rows 3 and 4 of back neck shaping.

Bind off all sts.

Sleeve (make 2)
With larger needles, cast on 46 (50, 54) sts; change to smaller needles.

Ribbing:
Row 1 (right side):
* K1, P1; rep from * across.

Rep Row 1 until sleeve measures 3", ending by working a right side row.

Next Row:
Rep Row 1, inc 22 sts evenly spaced across row—68 (72, 76) sts.

Change to larger size needles.

Body:
Row 1 (foundation row):
(K1, P1) 3 (4, 5) times—Seed St; P2, CF over next 6 sts; P5, K1 in st below, P5; Double Cable patt over next 18 sts; P5, K1 in st below, P5; CB over next 6 sts; P2, (K1, P1) 3 (4, 5) times—Seed St.

Row 2 and all even numbered rows:
Keeping to patt on Seed St, knit all other knit sts, and purl all other purl sts.

Referring to Pattern Stitches on pages 32 and 33, continue in patt, inc at each end every 4th row, keeping the inc sts in Seed St patt, until there are 108 (116, 124) sts on needle.

Work even (without inc) until sleeve measures 18" (19", 20").

Bind off all sts.

Hold front and back with right sides tog; with tapestry needle and yarn, sew shoulder seams.

Neckband:
With size 16" circular needle, beg at center back, pick up an even number of sts evenly spaced around neck.

Rnd 1:
* K1, P1; rep from * around.

Rep Rnd 1 until neckband measures about 2".
Bind off loosely in ribbing.

Finishing
Step 1:
Fold neckband to inside. With tapestry needle and yarn, sew bound-off edge to inside of row where stitches were picked up.

Step 2:
With right sides together, sew sleeves to body matching center of last row of sleeves to shoulder seams.

Step 3:
Sew side and sleeve seams. Weave in all ends.

Heather Cables

designed by Sandy Scoville

There's not an hombre around that wouldn't love this hand knit sweater, classicly styled with cables in ombre yarn.

Sizing:

Note: Instructions are written for size small; changes for larger sizes are in parentheses.

Size:	Small	Medium	Large
Chest Measurement:	36"-38"	42"-42"	44"-46"
Finished Chest Measurement:	42"	46"	50"

Materials:

Mohair-type worsted weight yarn, 14 (15, 16) oz [1300 (1400, 1500) yds, 400 (450, 500) g] red ombre

Size 8 straight or 24" circular knitting needles (your preference), or size required for gauge

Size 6 straight or 24" circular knitting needles (your preference)

Size 6, 16" circular knitting needle (for neckband)

Cable needle

Safety pins (optional)

Size 16 tapestry needle

Gauge:

With larger size needles, 4 sts = 1" in stockinette stitch (knit one row, purl one row)

Pattern Stitch

Cable (over 12 sts):

Row 1 (right side):
Knit.

Row 2 and all even numbered rows:
Purl.

Row 3:
Knit.

Row 5:
Sl 4 sts onto cable needle, hold in front of work, K4, K4 from cable needle; K4.

Rows 7, 9, and 11:
Knit.

Row 13:
K4, sl next 4 sts onto cable needle, hold in back of work, K4, K4 from cable needle.

Row 15:
Knit.

Row 16:
Purl.

Rep Rows 1 through 16 for patt.

Instructions

Note: When using circular needles, work back and forth in rows.

Back

With larger size needles, cast on 114 (120, 126) sts; change to smaller needles.

Ribbing:

Row 1 (right side):
* K1, P1; rep from * across.

Rep Row 1 until back measures 3". Change to larger size needles.

Body

Note: When working foundation row, refer to Pattern Stitch.

Row 1 (foundation row):
P3 (3, 6); † K12 (Cable patt), P6 †; rep from † to † once more; K12 (Cable patt), P12 (18, 18); rep from † to † twice; K12 (Cable patt), P3 (3, 6).

continued

Row 2:
Keeping to patt on cable sts, knit all other knit sts and purl all other purl sts.

Rep twisting cable on Row 5 and on every 8th row thereafter (see Cable patt on page 35) until back measures 24½" (25", 25"), ending by working a wrong side row.

Neck Shaping:
Note: Both shoulders are worked at the same time with separate skeins of yarn.

Row 1 (dividing row):
On first shoulder, work in patt across 42 (45, 48) sts; join second skein of yarn; bind off center 30 sts; on second shoulder, work in patt across.

Row 2:
Work in patt across both shoulders.

Row 3:
Work in patt to last 2 sts of first shoulder; K2 tog; on second shoulder, sl 1 as to knit, K1, PSSO, work in patt across.

Row 4:
Rep Row 2.

Bind off all sts.

Front
Work same as for back, working 10 rows less than back to neck shaping, ending by working a wrong side row.

Neck Shaping:
Row 1 (dividing row):
On first shoulder, work in patt across 45 (48, 51) sts; join second skein of yarn; bind off center 24 sts; on second shoulder, work in patt across.

Row 2:
Work in patt across both shoulders.

Row 3:
Work in patt to last 2 sts of first shoulder; K2 tog; on second shoulder, sl 1 as to knit, K1, PSSO, work in patt across.

Rows 4 through 9:
Rep Rows 2 and 3 three times.

Row 10:
Rep Row 2.

Bind off all sts.

Sleeve (make 2)
With larger size needles, cast on 34 (38, 42) sts; change to smaller size needles.

Ribbing:
Row 1 (right side):
* K1, P1; rep from * across.

Rep Row 1 until sleeve measures 3", ending by working a right side row.

Next Row:
Rep Row 1, inc 24 sts evenly spaced across row—58 (62, 66) sts.

Change to larger size needles.

Body:
Row 1:
P14 (16, 18); K12 (Cable patt), P6, K12 (Cable patt), P14 (16, 18).

Row 2:
Knit the knit sts and purl the purl sts.

Continue in patt, inc 1 st at each end every 4th row 17 (19, 21) times—92 (100, 108) sts.

Work even (without inc) until sleeve measures 18" (19", 20").

Bind off all stitches.

Hold front and back with right sides tog; with tapestry needle and yarn, sew shoulder seams.

Neckband:
With size 16" circular needle, and beg at center back, pick up even number of sts evenly spaced around neck.

Rnd 1:
* K1, P1; rep from * around.

Rep Rnd 1 until neckband measures about 1½".

Bind off loosely in ribbing.

Finishing
Step 1:
With right sides together, sew sleeves to body, matching centers of last row of sleeves to shoulder seams.

Step 2:
Sew side and sleeve seams. Weave in all ends.

Heather Stripe Knee Socks

designed by Sandy Scoville

When the weather turns frigid, your loved ones will appreciate the warmth and love that went into these hand-knit socks.

Sizes:
Note: Instructions are written for smaller size; changes for larger size are in parentheses.
Adult 9½" and 10½"

Materials:
Worsted weight wool or wool-blend yarn, 3 oz **(132 yds, 52 g)** each, rose and purple
Size 6, 7" double-pointed knitting needles, or size required for gauge
Stitch holder
Size 16 tapestry needle

Gauge:
11 sts = 2" in stockinette stitch **(knit one row, purl one row)**

Instructions

Socks (make 2)
Note: Change color by bringing new color under old color to prevent holes. Unless otherwise indicated, carry unused color along joining.

With rose, cast on 44 **(48)** sts; divide by placing first 14 **(16)** sts on one needle, 16 sts on second needle, and 14 **(16)** sts on third needle; join, being careful not to twist sts (see Special Techniques on page 6).

Note: Mark first st with contrasting color for beg of rnd.

Rnd 1 (right side):
* K1, P1; rep from * around.

Rnds 2 through 6:
Rep Rnd 1.

Calf:
Knit in stripe pattern as follows:

- ❑ purple, 2 rnds
- ❑ rose, 2 rnds
- ❑ purple, 2 rnds
- ❑ rose, 2 rnds
- ❑ purple, 1 rnd
- ❑ rose, 1 rnd
- ❑ purple, 1 rnd
- ❑ rose, 1 rnd

Rep stripe pattern until sock measures about 12" (13"), ending by working a rose rnd.

Cut both colors.

Heel:
Sl last 12 **(14)** sts of last rnd onto free needle; sl first 12 **(14)** sts of last rnd onto same needle; slip rem 20 sts onto a stitch holder for instep.

With wrong side facing you, join purple in first st.

Row 1 (wrong side):
Sl 1 as to purl, P23 **(27)**. Turn.

Row 2 (right side):
Sl 1 as to knit, knit rem sts. Turn.

Row 3:
Sl 1 as to purl, purl rem sts. Turn.

Row 4:
Rep Row 2.

Rep Rows 3 and 4 until heel measures about 2¼" **(2½")**, ending by working a right side row.

Turning Heel:
Row 1 (wrong side):
P15 **(17)**, P2 tog; P1. Turn, leaving rem sts unworked.

Row 2 (right side):
Sl 1 as to knit, K7 **(9)**, sl 1 as to knit, K1, PSSO; K1. Turn, leaving rem sts unworked.

Row 3:
Sl 1 as to purl, P8 **(10)**, P2 tog; P1. Turn, leaving rem sts unworked.

Row 4:
Sl 1 as to knit, K9 **(11)**, sl 1 as to knit, K1, PSSO; K1. Turn, leaving rem sts unworked.

continued

Heather Stripe Knee Socks *(continued)*

Row 5:
Sl 1 as to purl, P10 (12), P2 tog; P1. Turn, leaving rem sts unworked.

Row 6:
Sl 1 as to knit, K11 (13), sl 1 as to knit, K1, PSSO; K1. Turn, leaving rem sts unworked.

Row 7:
Sl 1 as to purl, P12 (14), P2 tog; P1. Turn.

Row 8:
Sl 1 as to knit, K13 (15), sl 1 as to knit, K1, PSSO; K1—16 (18) sts.

With right side facing you, on first needle, pick up 11 (13) sts along left side of heel; on second needle, knit 20 sts from stitch holder; on third needle, pick up 11 (13) sts along right side of heel; knit first 8 (9) sts of heel onto same needle; sl rem 8 (9) sts of heel onto beg of first needle—58 (64) sts. Cut yarn.

Foot:
Rnd 1:
Keeping to stripe pattern as established, join yarn, on first needle, knit to last 3 sts; K2 tog; K1; on second needle, K20; on third needle, K1, sl 1 as to knit, K1, PSSO; knit rem sts.

Rnd 2:
Knit.

Rnds 3 through 14 (20):
Rep Rows 1 and 2, 6 (9) times—44 sts.

Continuing in stripe pattern, knit even until foot measures 6¼" (7") from picked up sts at heel. Cut rose.

Toe Shaping:
Rnds 1 through 4:
With purple, rep Rnds 1 and 2 of foot twice—40 sts.

Rnd 5:
On first needle, knit to last 3 sts; K2 tog; K1; on second needle, K1, sl 1 as to knit, K1, PSSO; knit to last 3 sts; K2 tog; K1; on third needle, K1, sl 1 as to knit, K1, PSSO; knit rem sts.

Rnd 6:
Knit.

Rnds 7 through 14:
Rep Rnds 5 and 6, 4 times—20 sts.

Knit sts from first needle onto third needle.

Finishing
With tapestry needle and purple, weave toe together (see Special Techniques on page 6). Weave in all ends.

Heavenly

A glamorous Shetland lace design to rely on to top elegant evening wear or more casual on-the-town ensembles—will make the wearer feel just heavenly!

Size:
About 45" x 52" with edging

Materials:
Baby weight yarn, 14 oz (2380 yds, 420 g) ecru
Size 10, 36" circular knitting needle, or size required for gauge
Note: Circular needle is used to accomodate large number of stitches. Shawl in worked back and forth in rows.
Size 18 tapestry needle

Gauge:
10 sts = 2" in Lace Stitch

Pattern Stitch

Lace Stitch:
Row 1 (wrong side):
K1; ✱ P9, K1; rep from ✱ across.

Row 2 (right side):
P1; ✱ K3, YO, sl 1 as to knit, K2 tog; PSSO; YO, K3, P1; rep from ✱ across.

Row 3:
Purl.

Row 4:
K1; * YO, K3, sl 1 as to knit, K2 tog; PSSO; K3, YO, K1; rep from * across.

Row 5:
Purl.

Row 6:
P1; * K1, YO, K2, sl 1 as to knit, K2 tog; PSSO; K2, YO, K1, P1; rep from * across.

Row 7:
K1; * P9, K1; rep from * across.

Row 8:
P1; * K2, YO, K1, sl 1 as to knit, K2 tog; PSSO; K1, YO, K2, P1; rep from * across.

Rep Rows 1 through 8 for patt.

Instructions

Center
Cast on 201 sts. Do not join; work back and forth in rows.

Foundation Row:
Knit.

Rep Rows 1 through 8 of Lace Stitch pattern until piece measures about 38". Then rep Rows 1 and 2 once.

Loosely bind off.

Edging (make 4)
Note: Edging is worked separately in 4 pieces; then sewn to center and joined at corners.

Cast on 283 sts. Do not join; work back and forth in rows.

Row 1 (right side):
K1 tbl; * P2, K1 tbl; rep from * across.

Row 2:
P1; * K1 tbl, K1, P1; rep from * across.

Rep Rows 1 and 2 until piece measures 2½", ending by working a Row 2.

Now work 3 rows as follows:

Row 1:
K1 tbl; * drop next st off needle, P1, K1 tbl; rep from * across.

Row 2:
P1; * K1 tbl, P1; rep from * across.

Row 3:
K1 tbl; * P1, K1 tbl; rep from * across.

Loosely bind off.

Unravel each dropped st all the way down to the cast-on edge.

Finishing
Hold shawl and edging pieces with wrong sides together. Sew bound-off edge of edging pieces to sides of shawl. Weave ends of edging together at corners. Weave in all ends.

Honey, It's Cold!

It may be cold, but your little cutie won't notice in this cozy hat and mitten set—styled for girls or boys!

Sizes:
Note: Instructions are written for size small; changes for larger sizes are in parentheses.

Small	**Medium**	**Large**
(2-4)	(6-8)	(10-12)

Materials:
Worsted weight yarn, *for hat*, 3 (4, 5) oz [210 (280, 350) yds; 90 (120, 150) g] med blue; ½ oz (35 yds, 15 g) each lt green, lt purple, lt blue, white, med purple and med green; *for mittens*, 3 (3, 4) oz [210 (210, 280) yds, 90 (90, 120) g] med blue; ½ oz (35 yds, 15 g) each lt green, lt purple, lt blue, white, med purple and med green

Size 7 straight knitting needles, or size required for gauge

Size 5 straight knitting needles

Stitch holder

Markers

Size 16 tapestry needle

Gauge:
With larger size needles, 9 sts = 2" in stockinette stitch (knit one row, purl one row)

7 rows = 1"

Hat Instructions
With larger size needles and med blue, cast on 85 (90, 95) sts.

continued

Row 1 (right side):
Knit.

Row 2:
Purl.

Rep Rows 1 and 2 until piece measures 3", then continue to rep Rows 1 and 2 in following color sequence:

❑ lt green, 2 rows

❑ lt purple, 2 rows

❑ lt blue, 2 rows

❑ white, 2 rows

❑ med blue, 2 rows

❑ med purple, 2 rows

❑ med green, 2 rows

With med blue, continue to rep Rows 1 and 2 until piece measures 15" (16", 17"), ending with a wrong side row.

Shaping
Row 1:
 * K2 tog; K3; rep from * across—68 (72, 76) sts.

Row 2:
Purl.

Row 3:
* K2 tog; K2; rep from * across—51 (54, 57) sts.

Row 4:
Purl.

Row 5:
* K2 tog; K1; rep from * across—34 (36, 38) sts.

Row 6:
Purl.

Row 7:
* K2 tog; rep from * across—17 (18, 19) sts.

Cut yarn, leaving a 24" end.

Finishing
Step 1:
Thread end into tapestry needle and draw through all stitches. Draw up tightly and fasten securely.

Step 2:
Sew side seam, carefully matching stripes. Turn cast-on edge to inside to form a 5½" hem; slip stitch in place. Turn 3" of hem to outside to form striped cuff. Weave in all ends.

Mitten Instructions

Cuff
With smaller size needles and med blue, cast on 24 (28, 32) sts.

Row 1 (right side):
* K1, P1; rep from * across.

Row 2:
Rep Row 1.

Row 3:
With lt green, knit.

Row 4:
* K1, P1; rep from * across.

Rep Rows 3 and 4 in following color sequence:

❑ lt purple, 2 rows

❑ lt blue, 2 rows

❑ white, 2 rows

❑ med blue, 2 rows

❑ med purple, 2 rows

❑ med green, 2 rows

❑ med blue, 2 rows

Continuing with med blue, rep Row 1 until piece measures 2½" (3", 3½"), ending by working a wrong side row.

Change to larger size needles.

Palm
Row 1 (right side):
K2, inc (knit in front and back of next st); knit to last 3 sts; inc; K2—26 (30, 34) sts.

Row 2:
Purl.

Row 3:
Knit.

Row 4:
Purl.

Rep Rows 3 and 4 until piece measures 1" (2", 2½") from end of cuff.

Thumb Gusset:
Row 1:
K12 (14, 16); place marker on needle; inc twice; place marker on needle; K12 (14, 16).

Row 2:
Purl.

Row 3:
Knit to first marker; slip marker, inc; knit to last st before next marker; inc; slip marker; knit to end of row.

Rep Rows 2 and 3 until there are 8 (10, 12) sts between markers.

Hand
Row 1:
K12 (14, 16), drop marker; slip 8 (10, 12) thumb sts onto a stitch holder, drop marker; K12 (14, 16)—24 (28, 32) sts.

Row 2:
Purl.

Row 3:
Knit.

Row 4:
Purl.

Rep Rows 3 and 4 until piece measures 4" (5¹/₂", 6¹/₂").

Hand Shaping:
Row 1:
* K2, K2 tog; rep from * across—18 (21, 24) sts.

Row 2:
Purl.

Row 3:
* K1, K2 tog; rep from * across—12 (14, 16) sts.

Row 4:
Purl.

Row 5:
* K2 tog; rep from * 5 (6, 7) times more. Cut yarn, leaving an 18" end. Thread end into tapestry .needle and draw through all sts. Draw up tightly and fasten securely. Leave end for sewing.

Thumb
Slip sts from holder to larger size needle.

Row 1:
Knit.

Row 2:
Purl.

Rep Rows 1 and 2 until thumb measures 1¹/₄" (1¹/₂", 2 ") from end of gusset.

Next Row:
* K2 tog; rep from * 3 (4, 5) times more. Cut yarn, leaving a 12" end. Thread end into tapestry needle and draw through all sts. Draw up tightly and fasten securely. Leave end for sewing.

Work other mitten in same manner.

Finishing

Fold mitten lengthwise with wrong sides together; with long end, weave edges together from top of mitten to cuff. With yarn end at top of thumb, weave thumb seam. Weave in all ends.

Hound's Check

Even if it's a bit nippy outside, Buddy will still enjoy checking out his neighborhood beat wearing this fashionable houndstooth check coat.

Sizing:
Note: Instructions are written for size small; changes for larger sizes are in parentheses.

Size:	Small	Medium	Large
Length (base of tail to neck):	10"	14"	20"
Width (without side tabs):	9"	12"	18"

Materials:
Worsted weight yarn, 2 (3, 6) oz [140 (210, 420) yds; 60 (90, 180) g] each, red and gray
Size 10, 14" straight knitting needles, or size required for gauge
One 4" stitch holder
5/8"-wide hook and loop fastener such as Velcro®, 12" piece
Straight pins
Sewing needle and matching thread

Gauge:
19 sts = 4" in patt st

Pattern Stitch
Row 1:
With gray, * K1, yb, sl 1 as to purl; rep from * to last st; K1.

Row 2:
Knit. Drop gray.

Row 3:
With red, K2; * yb, sl 1 as to purl, K1; rep from * to last st; K1.

Row 4:
Knit. Drop red.

Rep Rows 1 through 4 for patt.

Instructions
Note: Carry colors along side of work.

With red, cast on 19 (25, 45) sts. Drop red; do not cut.

Row 1 (right side):
With gray, * K1, yb, sl 1 as to purl; rep from * to last st; K1.

Row 2:
Inc in first st (knit in front and back of st); knit to last 2 sts; inc in next st; K1—21 (27, 47) sts. Drop gray; do not cut.

Rows 3 and 4:
With red, rep Rows 1 and 2. At end of Row 4—23 (29, 49) sts. Drop red.

Rep Rows 1 through 4, 5 (7, 9) times more. At end of last row—43 (57, 85) sts.

Work even in patt st (beg with Row 1) until piece measures 10" (14", 20"), ending by working a Row 3.

Dividing Row:
With red, K14 (17, 25), sl these sts onto a stitch holder for shoulder; bind off next 15 (23, 35) sts for neck opening; knit rem sts for other shoulder. Drop red.

First Shoulder Shaping:
Row 1:
With gray, K1; * yb, sl 1 as to purl, K1; rep from * to last 2 sts; K2 tog—13 (16, 24) sts.

Row 2:
Knit. Drop gray.

Row 3:
With red, K2; * yb, sl 1 as to purl, K1; rep from * to last 2 sts; K2 tog—12 (15, 23) sts.

Row 4:
Knit. Drop red.

Work in patt st (beg with Row 1) until shoulder measures about 2" (3", 4") from bound-off sts at neck opening, ending by working a Row 3.

End Shaping:
Row 1 (wrong side):
With red, knit to last 2 sts; K2 tog—11 (14, 22) sts. Drop red.

Row 2 (right side):
With gray, K2 tog; * yb, sl 1 as to purl, K1; rep from * across—10 (13, 21) sts.

Row 3:
Knit to last 2 sts; K2 tog—9 (12, 20) sts. Drop gray.

Row 4:
With red, K2 tog; K1; * yb, sl 1 as to purl, K1; rep from * to last st; K1—8 (11, 19) sts.

Row 5:
Rep Row 3—7 (10, 18) sts. Drop red.

Row 6:
Rep Row 2—6 (9, 17) sts.

Row 7:
Rep Row 3—5 (8, 16) sts. Cut gray.

Row 8:
Rep Row 4—4 (7, 15) sts.

Bind off all sts.

Second Shoulder Shaping:
Hold piece with right side facing you; slip sts from holder to needle; join gray at left neck edge.

Row 1 (right side):
K2 tog; K1; * yb, sl 1 as to purl, K1; rep from * across—13 (16, 24) sts.

Row 2:
Knit. Drop gray.

Row 3:
With red, K2 tog; K1; * yb, sl 1 as to purl, K1; rep from * to last st; K1—12 (15, 23) sts.

Row 4:
Knit. Drop red.

Work even in patt st (beg with Row 1) until shoulder measures about 2" (3", 4") from bound-off sts at neck opening, ending by working a Row 3.

End Shaping:
Row 1 (wrong side):
With red, K2 tog; knit rem sts—11 (14, 22) sts. Drop red.

Row 2 (right side):
With gray, K1; * yb, sl 1 as to purl, K1; rep from * to last 3 sts; yb, sl 1 as to purl, K2 tog—10 (13, 21) sts.

Row 3:
K2 tog; knit rem sts—9 (12, 20) sts. Drop gray.

Row 4:
With red, K2; * yb, sl 1 as to purl, K1; rep from * to last 2 sts; K2 tog—8 (11, 19) sts.

Row 5:
Rep Row 3—7 (10, 18) sts. Drop red.

Row 6:
Rep Row 2—6 (9, 17) sts.

Row 7:
Rep Row 3—5 (8, 16) sts. Cut gray.

Row 8:
Rep Row 4—4 (7, 15) sts.

Bind off all sts.

Side Tab (make 2)
With right side facing you, mark with pins center 2" (4", 6") along side edge between neck opening and last increase row.

With gray, pick up 11 (19, 29) sts along center marked edge.

Next Row (wrong side):
Knit. Drop gray.

Work even in patt st (beg with Row 3) until tab measures about 2" (3", 4") from side edge or desired length, ending by working a Row 3.

End Shaping:
Row 1 (wrong side):
With red, K2 tog; knit to last 2 sts; K2 tog—9 (17, 27) sts. Drop red.

Row 2 (right side):
With gray, K2 tog; * yb, sl 1 as to purl, K1; rep from * to last 3 sts; yb, sl 1 as to purl, K2 tog—7 (15, 25) sts.

Row 3:
K2 tog; knit to last 2 sts; K2 tog—5 (13, 23) sts.

Small and Medium Sizes Only:
Cut gray.

Row 4:
With red, K2 tog; K1; * yb, sl 1 as to purl, K1; rep from * to last 2 sts; K2 tog—3 (11) sts.

Bind off all sts.

Large Size Only:
Row 4:
With red, K2 tog; K1; * yb, sl 1 as to purl, K1; rep from * to last 2 sts; K2 tog—21 sts.

Row 5:
K2 tog; knit to last 2 sts; K2 tog—19 sts. Drop red.

continued

Hound's Check *(continued)*

Row 6:
With gray, K2 tog; * yb, sl 1 as to purl, K1; rep from * to last 3 sts; yb, sl 1 as to purl, K2 tog—17 sts.

Row 7:
K2 tog; knit to last 2 sts; K2 tog—15 sts. Cut gray.

Row 8:
With red, K2 tog; * K1, yb, sl 1 as to purl; rep from * to last 3 sts; K1, K2 tog—13 sts.

Bind off all sts.

Finishing

Weave in all ends. Sew 4" pieces of hook and loop fastener at shoulder edges and side tab edges to close coat on front of chest and under stomach.

In Vest for Kids

designed by Kathy Wesley

The classic cable vest style is updated here for today's active playground set. A wonderful style for boys and girls!

Sizing:

Instructions are written for size small; changes for larger sizes are in parentheses.

Size:	Small (1-2)	Medium (3-4)	Large (5-6)
Finished Chest Measurement:	22"	28"	32"

Materials:

Worsted weight yarn, 6 (8, 10) oz [420 (560, 700) yds, 180 (240, 300) g] blue
Size 8 straight knitting needles, or size required for gauge
Size 6 straight knitting needles
Size 6, 16" circular knitting needle (for neckband)
One 4" stitch holder
Markers
Size 16 tapestry needle

Gauge:

With larger size needles, 6 sts = 1" in patt st
6 rows = 1"

Pattern Stitch

Mock Cable:

Row 1 (right side):
P2; * K1, P2, skip next st, K1 without removing st from needle, knit skipped st, slip both sts off needle—mock cable made; P2; rep from * to last 3 sts; K1, P2.

Row 2:
K2, P1; * K2, P2, K2, P1; rep from * to last 2 sts; K2.

Row 3:
P2; * K1, P2, K2, P2; rep from * to last 3 sts; K1, P2.

Row 4:
K2, P1; * K2, P2, K2, P1; rep from * to last 2 sts; K2.

Rep Rows 1 through 4 for patt.

Instructions

Back

With smaller size needles, cast on 67 (81, 95) sts.

Row 1 (wrong side):
K1; * P1, K1; rep from * across.

Row 2 (right side):
P1; * K1, P1; rep from * across.

Rep Rows 1 and 2 until ribbing measures 1½".

Row 3:
* K1, P1; rep from * to last st; inc (knit in front and back of next st)—68 (82, 96) sts.

Change to larger size needles. Work in mock cable patt (see Pattern Stitch) until piece measures 7" (8", 9"), ending by working a wrong side row.

Armhole Shaping:

Row 1:
Bind off 5 (5, 6) sts; work in patt across.

Row 2:
Bind off 5 (5, 6) sts; work in patt across—58 (72, 84) sts.

Row 3:
K1, K2 tog; work in patt to last 3 sts; sl 1 as to knit, K1, PSSO; K1.

Row 4:
Work in patt across.

Rep Rows 3 and 4, 2 (2, 3) times—52 (66, 76) sts.

Continue in patt until armhole measures 6½" (7", 7½"), ending by working a wrong side row.

Neckline Shaping:
Row 1:
For first shoulder, K1, K2 tog; work in patt over next 23 (30, 37) sts; sl 1 as to knit, K1, PSSO; K1; for second shoulder, join second skein of yarn; K1, K2 tog; work in patt to last 3 sts; sl 1 as to knit, K1, PSSO; K1.

Row 2:
Work in patt across both shoulders.

Row 3:
K1, K2 tog; work in patt to last 3 sts of first shoulder; sl 1 as to knit, K1, PSSO; K1; for second shoulder, K1, K2 tog; work in patt to last 3 sts; sl 1 as to knit, K1, PSSO; K1.

Row 4:
Work in patt across both shoulders.

Rep Rows 3 and 4, 1 (1, 2) times— 23 (30, 35) sts.

Row 5:
On first shoulder, work in patt to last 3 sts, sl 1 as to knit, K1, PSSO; K1; for second shoulder, K1, K2 tog; work in patt across.

Row 6:
Work in patt across both shoulders.

Rows 7 through 22 (28, 32):
Rep Rows 5 and 6. At end of Row 22 (28, 32)—14 (18, 21) sts.

Work even in patt (without dec) until armhole measures same as back to shoulder shaping, ending by working a wrong side row.

Shoulder Shaping:
Row 1:
Bind off 7 (9, 11) sts; work in patt across.

Row 2:
Bind off 7 (9, 11) sts; work in patt across.

Row 3:
Bind off 7 (9, 10) sts; work in patt across.

Bind off all sts.

Sew shoulder seams.

Neckband
Hold back with right side facing you; knit 24 (30, 34) sts from holder, pick up 24 (26, 28) sts along left front edge,

Shoulder Shaping:
Row 1:
Bind off 7 (9, 11) sts; work in patt across.

Row 2:
Bind off 7 (9, 11) sts; work in patt across.

Row 3:
Bind off 7 (9, 10) sts; work in patt across.

Row 4:
Bind off 7 (9,10) sts; work in patt across.

Place rem 24 (30, 34) sts onto a stitch holder for neckline.

Front
Work same as back to armhole.

Armhole Shaping:
Row 1:
Bind off 5 (5, 6) sts; work in patt across.

Row 2:
Bind off 5 (5, 6) sts; work in patt across—58 (72, 84) sts.

continued

In Vest for Kids (continued)

place marker on needle, pick up 24 **(26, 28)** sts along right front edge, pick up one st in seam—73 **(83, 91)** sts.

Rnd 1:
* K1, P1; rep from * to 2 sts before marker; K2 tog; sl marker, sl 1 as to knit, K1, PSSO; P1; ** K1, P1; rep from ** to end of rnd.

Rnd 2:
* K1, P1; rep from * to st before marker; K1, sl marker; ** K1, P1; rep from ** to end of rnd.

Rnd 3:
* K1, P1; rep from * to 3 sts before marker; K2 tog; K1, sl marker; K1, sl 1 as to knit, K1, PSSO; P1; ** K1, P1; rep from ** to end of rnd.

Rnd 4:
* K1, P1; rep from * to 2 sts before marker; K2; sl marker; K1; ** K1, P1; rep from ** to end of rnd.

Rnd 5:
* K1, P1; rep from * to 2 sts before marker; K2 tog; sl marker; sl 1 as to knit, K1, PSSO; P1; ** K1, P1; rep from ** to end of rnd.

Rnd 6:
* K1, P1; rep from * to st before marker; K1; sl marker; ** K1, P1; rep from ** to end of rnd.

Bind off in ribbing.

Armhole Ribbing
Hold vest with right side facing you and one armhole edge at top; pick up 36 **(40, 44)** sts along armhole edge from underarm to shoulder seam, pick up one st in shoulder seam, pick up 36 **(40, 44)** sts along armhole edge from shoulder seam to underarm—73 **(81, 89)** sts.

Row 1 (wrong side**):**
K1; * P1, K1; rep from * across.

Row 2:
P1; * K1, P1; rep from * across.

Rows 3 and 4:
Rep Rows 1 and 2.

Row 5:
Rep Row 1.

Bind off in ribbing.

Rep for other armhole.

Finishing
Sew side seams. Weave in ends.

Just Ducky

Baby will love seeing these bright happy ducklings on his own little footsies.

Size:
About 4¼" from heel to toe

Materials:
Worsted weight yarn, 1 oz (70 yds, 30 g) yellow
Size 8 straight knitting needles, or size required for gauge
Size 16 tapestry needle

Trimmings:
Two 1½" yellow pompons
Four ¼" brown pompons
2" x 3" piece of orange felt
Hot glue or tacky craft glue

Gauge:
9 sts = 2" in stockinette stitch (knit one row, purl one row)

Instructions

Slipper (make 2)
Cast on 27 sts.

Row 1 (wrong side):
K2, sl 1 as to purl, (K1, sl 1) 3 times; yf, P9, yb, (sl 1 as to purl, K1) 3 times; sl 1 as to purl, K2.

Row 2 (right side):
Knit.

Rep Rows 1 and 2 until piece measures 2³/₄", ending by working a right side row.

Toe Ribbing:
Row 1 (wrong side):
P1; * K1, P1; rep from * across.

Row 2 (right side):
K1; * P1, K1; rep from * across.

Rep Rows 1 and 2 until piece measures 4", ending by working a right side row.

Next Row:
K1; * K2 tog; rep from * across—14 sts.

Next Row:
* P2 tog; rep from * across—7 sts.

Cut yarn, leaving an 8" end.

Finishing
Step 1:
Thread yarn end into tapestry needle; draw through sts. Pull tight and secure. With same yarn, sew edges of ribbing only together.

Step 2:
Sew cast-on edge together for back seam from top edge to beginning of stockinette stitch section; weave needle through edge of stockinette stitches. Pull tight and secure to form heel. Weave in all ends.

Step 3:
Referring to photo for placement, glue one yellow pompon to center front of each slipper.

Step 4:
For duck's face, cut out beak from orange felt using **Fig 1** as a template. Fold on dotted line and glue in place. Referring to photo for placement, glue two ¹/₄" pompons on each large pompon for eyes.

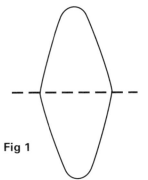

Fig 1

Leafy Stripes

Experienced knitters will enjoy the challenge of this lovely pattern stitch. Choose yarn in a favorite color and create a stunning beauty!

Sizing:
Note: Instructions are written for size small; changes for larger sizes are in parentheses.

Size:	Small	Medium	Large
Chest Measurement:	30"-32"	34"-36"	38"-40"
Finished Chest Measurement:	38"	42"	46"

Materials:
Worsted weight yarn, 12¹/₂ (13¹/₂, 14¹/₂) oz [1120 (1210, 1300) yds, 350 (380, 410) g] blue
Size 7 straight knitting needles, or size required for gauge
Markers
Safety pins (optional)
Size 16 tapestry needle

Gauge:
5 sts = 1" in stockinette stitch (knit one row, purl one row)

Pattern Stitch
Lace Pattern:
Row 1 (right side):
K1; * P4, K2 tog; K2, YO, K1, YO, K2, sl 1 as to knit, K1, PSSO; P4, K1; rep from * 4 (5, 6) times more.

Row 2:
P1; * K4, P9, K4, P1; rep from * across.

Row 3:
K1; * P4, K2 tog; K1, YO, K3, YO, K1, sl 1 as to knit, K1, PSSO; P4, K1; rep from * 4 (5, 6) times more.

Row 4:
Rep Row 2.

Row 5:
K1; * P4, K2 tog; YO, K5, YO, sl 1 as to knit, K1, PSSO; P4, K1; rep from * 4 (5, 6) times more.

Row 6:
Rep Row 2.

Rep Rows 1 through 6 for patt.

Instructions

Back/Front (make 2)
Cast on 91 (109, 127) sts.

Rows 1 and 2:
Knit.

continued

Leafy Stripes *(continued)*

Work Rows 1 through 6 of lace patt 19 **(20, 20)** times, or until piece measures 14" **(15", 15")**, ending by working a wrong side row.

Armhole Shaping:
Row 1:
Bind off 4 sts; work in patt across.

Row 2:
Bind off 4 sts; work in patt across.

Row 3:
Sl 1 as to knit, K1, PSSO; work in patt to last 2 sts; K2 tog.

Row 4:
Work in patt across.

Rows 5 and 6:
Rep Rows 3 and 4. At end of Row 6—79 **(97, 115)** sts.

Continue in patt until armhole shaping measures 2¼", ending by working a Row 6.

Yoke:
Row 1:

SMALL SIZE ONLY:
P1, inc **(knit in front and back of next st); *** P2, K2; rep from ***** 18 times more; P1—80 sts.

MEDIUM SIZE ONLY:
P1, K2 tog; K1; ***** P2, K2; rep from ***** 22 times more; P1—96 sts.

LARGE SIZE ONLY:
P1, inc **(knit in front and back of next st); *** P2, K2; rep from ***** 27 times more; P1—116 sts.

Row 2 (all sizes):
K1, P2; ***** K2, P2; rep from ***** 18 **(22, 27)** times more; K1.

Row 3:
P1, K2; ***** P2, K2; rep from ***** 18 **(22, 27)** times more; P1.

Row 4:
Rep Row 2.

Rep Rows 3 and 4 until armhole measures 8" **(8½", 9")** from beg of shaping.

Bind off in patt.

Sleeve **(make 2)**
Cast on 49 **(51, 53)** sts.

Rows 1 and 2:
Knit.

Row 3:
P15 **(16, 17)**; K1, P4, K2 tog; K2, YO, K1, YO, K2, sl 1 as to knit, K1, PSSO; P4, K1, P15 **(16, 17)**.

Row 4:
K15 **(16, 17)**; P1, K4, P9, K4, P1, K15 **(16, 17)**.

Row 5:
P15 **(16, 17)**; K1, P4, K2 tog; K1, YO, K3, YO, K1, sl 1 as to knit, K1, PSSO; P4, K1, P15 **(16, 17)**.

Row 6:
Rep Row 4.

Row 7:
P15 **(16, 17)**; K1, P4, K2 tog; YO, K5, YO, sl 1 as to knit, K1, PSSO; P4, K1, P15 **(16, 17)**.

Row 8:
Rep Row 4.

Rep Rows 3 through 8, inc in first and last st on every 4th row until there are 81 **(85, 89)** sts on needle. Work even **(without inc)** until sleeve measures 17" **(17½", 18")** from beg, ending by working a wrong side row.

Cap Shaping:
Row 1:
Bind off 4 sts; work in patt across.

Row 2:
Bind off 4 sts; work in patt across.

Row 3:
Sl 1 as to purl, P1, PSSO; work in patt to last 2 sts; P2 tog.

Row 4:
Work in patt across.

Rows 5 through 12:
Rep Rows 3 and 4 four times more. At end of Row 12—63 **(67, 71)** sts.

Rows 13 and 14:
Work in patt across.

Rows 15 and 16:
Rep Rows 3 and 4.

Rows 17 and 18:
Work in patt across.

Rep Rows 15 through 18 four times.

Last row:
* P2 tog; rep from * to last st; P1.

Bind off all sts.

Finishing
Step 1:
Sew shoulder seams, leaving 9" free on front and back for center neck opening.

Step 2:
Sew sleeves to body, matching centers of last row of sleeves to shoulder seams.

Step 3:
Sew sleeve and side seams. Weave in all ends.

Let's Go Visiting

Baby will be ready to enjoy the day, whether going to grandma's, baby playgroup or the grocery store.

Size:
3-6 months

Sweater:
Chest Measurement: 20"
Finished Chest Measurement: 21"

Materials:
Baby weight yarn, *for sweater*, 4 oz (680 yds, 120 g) white; 1 oz (170 yds, 30 g) each pink and green; *for bonnet*, 2 oz (340 yds, 60 g) white; ¼ oz (43 yds, 8 g) each pink and green
Size 5 straight knitting needles, or size required for gauge
Three 4" stitch holders
Size 18 tapestry needle
Five ½"-diameter white buttons
¾ yd of ⅜"-wide white satin ribbon
⅓ yd of ¼"-wide white satin ribbon
Sewing needle and matching thread

Gauge:
13 sts = 2" in stockinette stitch (knit one row, purl one row)
18 rows = 2"

Sweater Instructions

Back

Ribbing:
With white, cast on 67 sts.

Row 1 (right side):
K1; * P1, K1; rep from * across.

Row 2:
P1; * K1, P1; rep from * across.

Rows 3 through 8:
Rep Rows 1 and 2 three times.

Row 9:
Rep Row 1.

Row 10:
* P1, K1; rep from * to last st; inc (knit in front and back of next st)—68 sts.

Body:
Note: Change color by bringing new color under old color to prevent holes. Unless otherwise indicated, carry unused color along side.

Row 1:
Knit.

Row 2:
Purl. Cut white.

Row 3:
With pink, K1; * YO, K2 tog; rep from * to last st; K1.

Rows 4 through 6:
Rep Row 3.

Rows 7 and 8:
With green, rep Row 3.

Rows 9 through 12:
With pink, rep Row 3. At end of Row 12, cut pink and green.

Row 13:
With white, knit.

Row 14:
Purl.

Rep Rows 13 and 14 until piece measures 7", ending by working a wrong side row.

Armhole Shaping:
Row 1:
Bind off 4 sts; knit across.

Row 2:
Bind off 4 sts; purl across—60 sts.

continued

Row 3:
K1, K2 tog; knit to last 3 sts; sl 1 as to knit, K1, PSSO; K1—58 sts.

Row 4:
Purl.

Rows 5 through 8:
Rep Rows 3 and 4 twice—54 sts.

Row 9:
Knit.

Row 10:
Purl.

Rep Rows 9 and 10 until armhole measures $3^3/_4$", ending by working a wrong side row.

Shoulder Shaping:
Row 1:
Bind off 7 sts; knit across.

Row 2:
Bind off 7 sts; purl across.

Row 3:
Bind off 6 sts; knit across.

Row 4:
Bind off 6 sts; purl across.

Slip rem 28 sts onto a stitch holder for back neckline.

Left Front
Note: Buttonholes are worked on left front of sweater for boys; on right front for girls.

Ribbing:
With white, cast on 36 sts.

Row 1 (right side):
K1; * P1, K1; rep from * to last 5 sts; (K1, P1) twice; K1—front band made.

Row 2:
(K1, P1) twice; K1; * P1, K1; rep from * to last st; P1.

Row 3:
Rep Row 1.

Row 4 (for girls):
Rep Row 2.

Row 4 (for boys):
K1, P1, YO, P2 tog—buttonhole made; K1; * P1, K1; rep from * to last st; P1.

Rows 5 through 10:
Rep Rows 1 and 2 three times.

Body:
Row 1:
Knit to last 5 sts; (K1, P1) twice; K1.

Row 2:
(K1, P1) twice; K1; purl across. Cut white.

Row 3:
With pink, K1; * YO, K2 tog; rep from * to last 5 sts; with white, (K1, P1) twice; K1.

Row 4:
(K1, P1) twice; K1; with pink, * YO, K2 tog; rep from * to last st; K1.

Row 5:
K1; * YO, K2 tog; rep from * to last 5 sts; with white, (K1, P1) twice; K1.

Row 6:
(K1, P1) twice; K1; with pink, * YO, K2 tog; rep from * to last st; K1.

Row 7:
With green, K1; * YO, K2 tog; rep from * to last 5 sts; K1; with white, (K1, P1) twice; K1.

Row 8:
(K1, P1) twice; K1; with green, * YO, K2 tog; rep from * to last st; K1. Cut green.

Rows 9 through 12:
Rep Rows 3 through 6. At end of Row 12, cut pink.

Note: For boys, work 2nd and 3rd buttonholes 2" from last buttonhole made.

Row 13:
With white, knit to last 5 sts; (K1, P1) twice; K1.

Row 14:
(K1, P1) twice; K1; purl across.

Rep Rows 13 and 14 until piece measures same as back to armhole shaping.

Armhole Shaping:
Note: For boys, work 4th buttonhole 2" from last buttonhole made.

Row 1 (right side):
Bind off 4 sts, knit to last 5 sts; (K1, P1) twice; K1.

Row 2:
(K1, P1) twice; K1; purl across.

Row 3:
K1, K2 tog; knit to last 5 sts; (K1, P1) twice; K1.

Row 4:
(K1, P1) twice; K1; purl across.

Rows 5 through 8:
Rep Rows 3 and 4 twice—29 sts.

Row 9:
Knit to last 5 sts; (K1, P1) twice; K1.

Row 10:
(K1, P1) twice; K1; purl across.

Row 11:
Knit to last 5 sts; (K1, P1) twice; K1.

Rep Rows 10 and 11 until armhole measures 2".

Neck Shaping:
(K1, P1) twice; K1, P6; slip these 11 sts onto a stitch holder for front neckline; purl rem 18 sts.

Row 1 (right side):
Knit to last 3 sts; sl 1 as to knit, K1, PSSO; K1.

Row 2:
Purl.

Rows 3 through 10:
Rep Rows 1 and 2 four times— 13 sts.

Row 11:
Knit.

Row 12:
Purl.

Rep Rows 11 and 12 until front measures same as back to shoulder shaping.

Shoulder Shaping:
Row 1:
Bind off 7 sts; knit across.

Row 2:
Purl.

Bind off all sts.

Right Front
Ribbing:
With white, cast on 36 sts.

Row 1 (right side):
(K1, P1) twice; K1—front band made; * K1, P1; rep from * to last st; K1.

Row 2:
P1; * K1, P1; rep from * to last 5 sts; (K1, P1) twice; K1.

Row 3:
Rep Row 1.

Row 4 (for boys):
Rep Row 2.

Row 4 (for girls):
P1; * K1, P1; rep from * to last 5 sts; K1, P1, YO, P2 tog—buttonhole made; K1.

Rows 5 through 10:
Rep Rows 1 and 2 three times.

Body:
Row 1:
(K1, P1) twice; K1; knit across.

Row 2:
Purl to last 5 sts; (K1, P1) twice; K1.

Row 3:
(K1, P1) twice; K1; with pink, * YO, K2 tog; rep from * to last st; K1.

Row 4:
K1; * YO, K2 tog; rep from * to last 5 sts; with white, (K1, P1) twice; K1.

Rows 5 and 6:
Rep Rows 3 and 4.

Row 7:
(K1, P1) twice; K1; with green, * YO, K2 tog; rep from * to last st; K1.

continued

Row 8:
K1; * YO, K2 tog; rep from * to last 5 sts; with white, (K1, P1) twice; K1. Cut green.

Rows 9 through 12:
Rep Rows 3 through 6. At end of Row 12, cut pink.

Note: For girls, work 2nd and 3rd buttonholes 2" from last buttonhole made.

Row 13:
(K1, P1) twice; K1; knit across.

Row 14:
Purl to last 5 sts; (K1, P1) twice; K1.

Rep Rows 13 and 14 until piece measures same as back to armhole shaping.

Armhole Shaping:
Note: For girls, work 4th buttonhole 2" from last buttonhole made.

Row 1 (wrong side):
Bind off 4 sts; purl to last 5 sts; (K1, P1) twice; K1.

Row 2 (right side):
(K1, P1) twice; K1, knit to last 3 sts; sl 1 as to knit, K1, PSSO; K1.

Row 3:
Purl to last 5 sts; (K1, P1) twice; K1.

Rows 4 through 7:
Rep Rows 2 and 3 twice—29 sts.

Row 8:
(K1, P1) twice; K1; knit across.

Row 9:
Purl to last 5 sts; (K1, P1) twice; K1.

Rep Rows 8 and 9 until armhole measures 2".

Neck Shaping:
Row 1 (right side):
(K1, P1) twice; K1, P6; slip these 11 sts onto a stitch holder for front neckline; knit rem 18 sts.

Row 2:
Purl.

Row 3:
K1, K2 tog; knit across.

Rows 4 through 9:
Rep Rows 2 and 3 four times—13 sts.

Row 10:
Purl.

Row 11:
Knit.

Rep Rows 10 and 11 until front measures same as back to shoulder shaping.

Shoulder Shaping:
Row 1 (wrong side):
Bind off 7 sts; purl across.

Row 2 (right side):
Knit.

Bind off rem sts.

Sleeve (make 2)
Ribbing:
With white, cast on 33 sts.

Row 1 (right side):
K1; * P1, K1; rep from * across.

Row 2:
P1; * K1, P1; rep from * across.

Rep Rows 1 and 2 until piece measures 2".

Next Row:
* Inc; K3; rep from * 7 times more; inc—42 sts.

Body:
Row 1:
Knit.

Row 2:
Purl. Cut white.

Row 3:
With pink, K1; * YO, K2 tog; rep from * to last st; K1.

Rows 4 through 6:
Rep Row 3.

Rows 7 and 8:
With green, rep Row 3.

Rows 9 through 12:
With pink, rep Row 3. At end of Row 12, cut pink and green.

Row 13:
With white, inc; knit to last st; inc.

Row 14:
Purl.

Row 15:
Knit.

Row 16:
Purl.

Rows 17 and 18:
Rep Rows 15 and 16.

Rows 19 through 30:
Rep Rows 13 through 18 twice. At end of Row 30—48 sts.

Rep Rows 15 and 16 until sleeve measures 7½", ending by working a wrong side row.

Cap Shaping:
Row 1:
Bind off 4 sts; knit across.

Row 2:
Bind off 4 sts; purl across—40 sts.

Row 3:
K1, K2 tog; knit to last 3 sts; sl 1 as to knit, PSSO; K1.

Row 4:
Purl.

Rows 5 through 24:
Rep Rows 3 and 4 ten times—18 sts.

Bind off all sts.

Sew shoulder seams.

Neckband:
Row 1 (right side):
With right side facing you, slip 11 right front neckline sts from holder to needle, with white, pick up 15 sts along right front neck edge, K28 from back holder, pick up 14 sts along left front neck edge, work 11 left front neckline sts from holder as follows: K6, (K1, P1) twice; K1—79 sts.

Row 2:
* K1, P1; rep from * to last st; K1.

Row 3:
For front band, (K1, P1) twice; K1; for neckline ribbing, K1; * P1, K1; rep from * to last 5 sts; for front band, (K1, P1) twice; K1.

Row 4 (for boys):
K1, P1, YO, P2 tog—buttonhole made; K1; * P1, K1; rep from * across.

Row 4 (for girls):
* K1, P1; rep from * to last 3 sts; YO, P2 tog—buttonhole made; K1.

Row 5:
Rep Row 3.

Rows 6 and 7:
Rep Rows 2 and 3.

Bind off all sts.

Bonnet Instructions
Beg at front edge with white, cast on 67 sts.

Row 1 (right side):
K1; * P1, K1; rep from * across.

Row 2:
P1; * K1, P1; rep from * across.

Rows 3 through 6:
Rep Rows 1 and 2 twice.

Row 7:
K16; * K2 tog; K5; rep from * 4 times more; K16—62 sts.

Row 8:
Purl.

Row 9:
With pink, K1; * YO, K2 tog; rep from * to last st; K1.

Rows 10 through 18:
Rep Row 9 in following color sequence:

❏ pink, 3 rows

❏ green, 2 rows

❏ pink, 4 rows

Cut pink and green.

Row 19:
With white, knit.

Row 20:
Purl.

Rep Rows 19 and 20 until piece measures 4½".

Back Shaping:
Row 1 (right side):
K42, sl 1 as to knit, K1, PSSO; turn, leaving rem 18 sts unworked.

Row 2:
Sl 1 as to purl, P22, P2 tog; turn, leaving rem 18 sts unworked.

Row 3:
Sl 1 as to purl, K22, sl 1 as to knit, K1, PSSO; turn, leaving rem 17 sts unworked.

Row 4:
Sl 1 as to purl, P22, P2 tog; turn, leaving rem 17 sts unworked.

Row 5:
Sl 1 as to purl, K22, sl 1 as to knit, K1, PSSO; turn, leaving rem sts unworked.

Row 6:
Sl 1 as to purl, P22, P2 tog; turn, leaving rem sts unworked.

continued

Rows 7 through 34:
Rep Rows 5 and 6 fourteen times. At end of Row 34, turn, leaving rem 2 sts unworked.

Row 35:
Sl 1 as to purl, K22, sl 1 as to knit, K2 tog; PSSO; turn, leaving rem 2 sts unworked.

Row 36:
Sl 1 as to purl, P22, P3 tog—24 sts. Cut yarn, leaving sts on needle.

Neckband:
Hold piece with right side facing you and ends of rows at top. Join white in upper right-hand corner in edge of first row of ribbing. Working across neck edge, pick up 6 sts across ribbing, 6 sts across color pattern, and 18 sts across stock sts to back sts on needle; working across sts on needle, * sl 1 as to knit, K2 tog; PSSO; rep from * 7 times more; working across ends of rows, pick up 18 sts across stock sts, 6 sts across color pattern, and 6 sts across ribbing—68 sts.

Row 1 (wrong side):
(K1, P1) 6 times; (K2 tog, P2 tog) 3 times; (K1, P1) 4 times; K1, P2 tog; K1, (P1, K1) 4 times; (P2 tog, K2 tog) 3 times; (P1, K1) 6 times—55 sts.

Row 2:
P1; * K1, P1; rep from * across.

Row 3:
K1; * P1, K1; rep from * across.

Rows 4 and 5:
Rep Rows 2 and 3.

Bind off in ribbing.

Finishing
Step 1:
Sew sleeves to body, matching center of last row of sleeves to shoulder seams.

Step 2:
Sew side and sleeve seams.

Step 3:
Sew buttons opposite buttonholes.

Step 4:
For ties, cut ³/₈"-wide ribbon in half. Fold one end of each length under about ¹/₄" and pin a length to each side of Bonnet neck edge.

Step 5:
Cut ¹/₄"-wide ribbon in half. Tie each length into a small bow; trim ends. Pin bows to ties; sew bows and ties securely in place.

Northern Lights Mittens

These great fitting mittens are actually knitted on just two needles. They are shown in variegated yarn which is fun to knit with, because you never know exactly what pattern will appear.

Sizes:
Note: Instructions are written for smaller size; changes for larger size are in parentheses.
Women's glove size 5¹/₂-6¹/₂
Women's glove size 7-8¹/₂

Materials:
Worsted weight yarn, 3 (4) oz [210 (280) yds, 90 (120) g] variegated
Size 7 straight knitting needles, or size required for gauge
Size 5 straight knitting needles
One 4" stitch holder
Markers
Size 16 tapestry needle

Gauge
With larger side needles, 5 sts = 1" in stockinette stitch (knit one row, purl one row)
7 rows = 1"

Instructions

Mitten (make 2)

Cuff:
With smaller size needles, cast on 32 (36) sts.

Row 1:
* K1, P1; rep from * across.

Rep Row 1 until piece measures 5" (5¹/₂").

Change to larger size needles.

Palm:
Row 1 (right side):
K2, inc (knit in front and back of next st); knit to last 3 sts; inc; K2—34 (38) sts.

Row 2:
Purl.

Row 3:
Knit.

Row 4:
Purl.

Rep Rows 3 and 4 until piece measures 1" (1$\frac{1}{2}$") from end of ribbing, ending by working a wrong side row.

Thumb Gusset:
Row 1:
K16 (18), place marker on needle; inc twice; place marker on needle; K16 (18).

Note: Slip markers on each row.

Row 2:
Purl.

Row 3:
Knit to first marker; inc; knit to last st before next marker, inc; knit rem sts.

Row 4:
Purl.

Rep Rows 3 and 4 until there are 12 (14) sts between markers.

Hand:
Row 1:
K16 (18), remove marker; place 12 (14) thumb sts onto a stitch holder; remove marker, K16 (18).

Row 2:
Purl.

Row 3:
Knit.

Row 4:
Purl.

Rep Rows 3 and 4 until piece measures 6$\frac{1}{2}$" (7$\frac{1}{2}$") from top of ribbing, ending by working a Row 4.

Hand Shaping:
Row 1:
* K2, K2 tog; rep from * across—24 (27) sts.

Row 2:
Purl.

Row 3:
* K1, K2 tog; rep from * across—16 (18) sts.

Row 4:
Purl.

Row 5:
* K2 tog; rep from * across. Cut yarn, leaving an 18" end. Thread end into tapestry needle and draw needle through all sts. Draw up tightly and fasten securely. Leave end for sewing.

Thumb:
Slip sts from holder to larger size needle.

Work in stock st until thumb measures 2" (2$\frac{1}{4}$") from end of gusset, ending by working a purl row.

Next Row:
* K2 tog; rep from * across. Cut yarn, leaving a 12" end.

Thread end into tapestry needle and draw through all sts. Draw yarn up tightly and fasten securely. Leave end for sewing.

Work other mitten in same manner.

Finishing
Fold mitten. With yarn ends, sew seam from top of mitten to cuff; sew thumb seam. Weave in all ends.

Playtime For Baby

Size:
3 to 6 months
Chest Measurement: 20"
Finished Chest Measurement: 21"

Materials:
Baby weight yarn, 3½ oz (595 yds, 105 g) blue
Size 6 straight knitting needles, or size required for
    gauge
Size 4 straight knitting needles
Five 4" stitch holders
Markers
Size 18 tapestry needle
Six 1⅓"-diameter blue buttons
Sewing needle and matching thread

Gauge:
With larger size needles, 6 sts = 1" in stockinette stitch
    (knit one row, purl one row)
8 rows = 1"

Instructions

Back
With smaller size needles, cast on 63 sts.

Ribbing:
Row 1 (right side):
K1; * P1, K1; rep from * across.

Row 2:
P1; * K1, P1; rep from * across.

Rows 3 through 8:
Rep Rows 1 and 2.

Change to larger size needles.

Body:
Row 1 (right side):
Knit.

Row 2:
Purl.

Rows 3 through 40:
Rep Rows 1 and 2 nineteen times.

Armhole Shaping:
Row 1:
Bind off 4 sts; knit across.

56

Row 2:
Bind off 4 sts; purl across—55 sts.

Row 3:
K2, sl 1 as to knit, K1, PSSO; knit to last 4 sts; K2 tog; K2.

Row 4:
Purl.

Rows 5 through 34:
Rep Rows 3 and 4 fifteen times. Slip rem 23 sts onto a stitch holder for back of neck.

Left Front

Note: Buttonholes are worked on left front of sweater for boys; on right front for girls.

Ribbing:
With smaller size needles, cast on 37 sts.

Row 1 (right side)**:**
K1; * P1, K1; rep from * across.

Row 2:
P1; * K1, P1; rep from * across.

Rows 3 and 4:
Rep Rows 1 and 2.

Row 5 (for girls)**:**
Rep Row 1.

Row 5 (for boys)**:**
K1; * P1, K1; rep from * to last 6 sts; P1, K1, YO, K2 tog—buttonhole made; P1, K1.

Row 6:
Rep Row 2.

Rows 7 and 8:
Rep Rows 1 and 2.

Change to larger size needles.

Body:
Row 1 (right side)**:**
Knit to last 10 sts; P1, K3 (for mock cable); (P1, K1) 3 times (for front band).

Row 2:
(P1, K1) 3 times; P3, K1; purl rem sts.

Note: On following rows pass slipped stitch over both knitted stitches for mock cable (PSSO2).

Row 3:
Knit to last 10 sts; P1, sl 1 as to knit, K2, PSSO2; (P1, K1) 3 times.

Row 4:
(P1, K1) 3 times; P1, YO, P1, K1; purl rem sts.

Rows 5 through 8:
Rep Rows 1 through 4.

Row 9 (for girls)**:**
Rep Row 1.

Row 9 (for boys)**:**
Knit to last 10 sts; P1, K3, P1, K1, YO, K2 tog—buttonhole made; P1, K1.

Rows 10 through 12:
Rep Rows 2 through 4.

Rows 13 through 16:
Rep Rows 1 through 4.

Rows 17 and 18:
Rep Rows 1 and 2.

Row 19 (for girls)**:**
Rep Row 3.

Row 19 (for boys)**:**
Knit to last 10 sts; P1, sl 1 as to knit, K2, PSSO2; P1, K1, YO, K2 tog—buttonhole made; P1, K1.

Row 20:
Rep Row 4.

Rows 21 through 28:
Rep Rows 1 through 4 twice.

Row 29 (for girls)**:**
Rep Row 1.

Row 29 (for boys)**:**
Rep Row 9.

Rows 30 through 32:
Rep Rows 2 through 4:

Rows 33 through 36:
Rep Rows 1 through 4.

Rows 37 and 38:
Rep Rows 1 and 2.

Row 39 (for girls)**:**
Rep Row 3.

Row 39 (for boys)**:**
Rep Row 19.

Row 40:
Rep Row 4.

Armhole Shaping:
Row 1 (right side)**:**
Bind off 4 sts; knit to last 10 sts; P1, K3, (P1, K1) 3 times—33 sts.

Row 2:
(P1, K1) 3 times; P3, K1; purl rem sts.

continued

Row 3:
K2, sl 1 as to knit, K1, PSSO; knit to last 10 sts; P1, sl 1 as to knit, K2, PSSO2; (P1, K1) 3 times.

Row 4:
(P1, K1) 3 times; P1, K1, YO, P1; purl rem sts.

Row 5:
K2, sl 1 as to knit, K1, PSSO; knit to last 10 sts; P1, K3, (P1, K1) 3 times.

Rows 6 through 8:
Rep Rows 2 through 4.

Row 9 (for girls):
Rep Row 5.

Row 9 (for boys):
K2, sl 1 as to knit, K1, PSSO; knit to last 10 sts; P1, K3, P1, K1, YO, K2 tog; P1, K1—buttonhole made.

Rows 10 through 13:
Rep Rows 2 through 5. At end of Row 13—27 sts.

Row 14:
Rep Row 2.

Neckline Shaping:
Row 1:
K2, sl 1 as to knit, K1, PSSO; knit to last 10 sts; P1, K3, (P1, K1) 3 times.

Row 2:
(P1, K1) 3 times; P3, K1; slip these 10 sts onto a stitch holder for left front neckline; purl rem 16 sts.

Row 3:
K2, sl 1 as to knit, K1, PSSO; knit to last 3 sts; K2 tog; K1—14 sts.

Row 4:
Purl.

Rows 5 through 12:
Rep Rows 3 and 4 four times—6 sts.

Row 13:
K2, sl 1 as to knit, K1, PSSO; K2—5 sts.

Row 14:
Purl.

Rows 15 through 18:
Rep Rows 13 and 14 twice—3 sts.

Bind off all sts.

Right Front
Ribbing:
With smaller size needles, cast on 37 sts.

Row 1:
K1; * P1, K1; rep from * across.

Row 2:
P1; * K1, P1; rep from * across.

Rows 3 and 4:
Rep Rows 1 and 2.

Row 5 (for boys):
Rep Row 1.

Row 5 (for girls):
K1, P1, K1, YO, K2 tog—buttonhole made; * P1, K1; rep from * across.

Row 6:
Rep Row 2.

Rows 7 and 8:
Rep Rows 1 and 2.

Change to larger size needles.

Body:
Row 1 (right side):
(K1, P1) 3 times; K3, P1 (for mock cable); knit rem sts.

Row 2:
Purl to last 10 sts; K1, P3, (K1, P1) 3 times.

Row 3:
(K1, P1) 3 times; sl 1 as to knit, K2, PSSO2; P1; knit rem sts.

Row 4:
Purl to last 9 sts; K1, P1, YO, P1, (K1, P1) 3 times.

Rows 5 through 8:
Rep Rows 1 through 4.

Row 9 (for boys):
Rep Row 1.

Row 9 (for girls):
K1, P1, K1, YO, K2 tog; P1—buttonhole made; K3, P1; knit rem sts.

Rows 10 through 12:
Rep Rows 2 through 4.

Rows 13 through 16:
Rep Rows 1 through 4.

Rows 17 and 18:
Rep Rows 1 and 2.

Row 19 (for boys):
Rep Row 3.

Row 19 (for girls):
K1, P1, K1, YO, K2 tog; P1—buttonhole made; sl 1 as to knit, K2, PSSO2; P1; knit rem sts.

Row 20:
Rep Row 4.

Rows 21 through 28:
Rep Rows 1 through 4 twice.

Row 29 (for boys)**:**
Rep Row 1.

Row 29 (for girls)**:**
Rep Row 9.

Rows 30 through 32:
Rep Rows 2 through 4.

Rows 33 through 36:
Rep Rows 1 through 4.

Rows 37 and 38:
Rep Rows 1 and 2.

Row 39 (for boys)**:**
Rep Row 3.

Row 39 (for girls)**:**
Rep Row 19.

Row 40:
Rep Row 4.

Armhole Shaping:
Row 1 (right side)**:**
(K1, P1) 3 times; K3, P1; knit rem sts.

Row 2:
Bind off 4 sts; purl to last 10 sts; K1, P3, (K1, P1) 3 times—33 sts.

Row 3:
(K1, P1) 3 times; sl 1 as to knit, K2, PSSO2; P1; knit to last 4 sts; K2 tog; K2.

Row 4:
Purl to last 9 sts; K1, P1, YO, P1, (K1, P1) 3 times.

Row 5:
(K1, P1) 3 times; K3, P1; knit to last 4 sts; K2 tog; K2.

Row 6:
Purl to last 10 sts; K1, P3, (K1, P1) 3 times.

Rows 7 and 8:
Rep Rows 3 and 4.

Row 9 (for boys)**:**
Rep Row 5.

Row 9 (for girls)**:**
K1, P1, K1, YO, K2 tog; P1—buttonhole made; K3, P1; knit to last 4 sts; K2 tog; K2.

Row 10:
Purl to last 10 sts; K1, P3, (K1, P1) 3 times.

Rows 11 through 14:
Rep Rows 3 through 6. At end of Row 14—27 sts.

Neckline Shaping:
Row 1:
(K1, P1) 3 times; K3, P1; knit to last 4 sts; K2 tog; K2.

Row 2:
P16; slip rem 10 sts onto a stitch holder for right front neckline.

Row 3:
K1, sl 1 as to knit, K1, PSSO; knit to last 4 sts; K2 tog; K2—14 sts.

Row 4:
Purl.

Rows 5 through 12:
Rep Rows 3 and 4 four times.

Row 13:
K2, K2 tog; K2—5 sts.

Row 14:
Purl.

Rows 15 through 18:
Rep Rows 13 and 14 twice—3 sts.

Bind off all sts.

Sleeve (make 2)
With smaller size needles, cast on 37 sts.

Ribbing:
Row 1 (right side)**:**
K1; ✱ P1, K1; rep from ✱ across.

Row 2:
P1; ✱ K1, P1; rep from ✱ across.

Rep Rows 1 and 2 until piece measures 1½″, ending by working a Row 2.

Next Row:
Rep Row 1.

Next Row:
Inc (knit in front and back of next st); K1; ✱ P1, K1; rep from ✱ across to last st; inc—39 sts.

Change to larger size needles.

Body:
Row 1 (right side)**:**
K17; place marker; P1, K3, P1 (for mock cable); place marker; K17.

Note: Markers are used to separate cable pattern stitches. They are set in place on the first row, and should be

continued

moved from the left-hand needle to the right-hand needle as you come to them. They may be removed when you are familiar with the pattern.

Row 2:
P17, K1, P3, K1, P17.

Row 3:
Knit to first marker; P1, sl 1 as to knit, K2, PSSO2; P1; knit rem sts.

Row 4:
Purl to first marker; K1, P1, YO, P1, K1; purl rem sts.

Row 5:
K1, inc; knit to first marker; P1, K3, P1; knit to last 2 sts; inc; K1—41 sts.

Row 6:
Purl to first marker; K1, P3, K1; purl rem sts.

Rows 7 and 8:
Rep Rows 3 and 4.

Row 9:
Knit to first marker; P1, K3, P1; knit rem sts.

Row 10:
Rep Row 6.

Row 11:
Inc; knit to first marker; P1, sl 1 as to knit, K2, PSSO2; P1; knit to last st; inc.

Row 12:
Rep Row 4.

Row 13:
Rep Row 9.

Row 14:
Rep Row 6.

Rows 15 through 18:
Rep Rows 3 through 6. At end of Row 18—45 sts.

Rep Rows 7 through 10, until sleeve measures about 7¹⁄₂".

Armhole Shaping:
Row 1:
Bind off 4 sts; knit to first marker; P1, sl 1 as to knit, K2, PSSO2; knit rem sts.

Row 2:
Bind off 4 sts; purl to first marker; K1, P1, YO, P1, K1; purl rem sts—37 sts.

Row 3:
K2, sl 1 as to knit, K1, PSSO; knit to first marker; P1, K3, P1, knit to last 4 sts; K2 tog; K2—35 sts.

Row 4:
Purl to first marker; K1, P3, K1, purl rem sts.

Row 5:
K2, sl 1 as to knit, K1, PSSO; knit to first marker; P1, sl 1 as to knit, K2, PSSO2; knit to last 4 sts; K2 tog; K2—33 sts.

Row 6:
Purl to first marker; K1, P1, YO, P1, K1, purl rem sts.

Rep Rows 3 through 6 seven times—7 sts.

Next Row:
K2, sl 1, K2 tog; PSSO, K2—5 sts.

Next Row:
Purl.

Slip rem 5 sts onto a stitch holder.

Sew sleeves to body, carefully matching decreases. Sew side and sleeve seams.

Neckband
With right side facing you and smaller size needles, work across 10 sts on right front stitch holder as follows: **(K1, P1)** 5 times; pick up 15 sts along right front neck edge, K5 from right sleeve stitch holder, K23 from back stitch holder, K5 from left sleeve stitch holder, pick up 15 sts along left front neck edge; work across sts on left front stitch holder as follows: **(P1, K1)** 5 times—83 sts.

Row 2:
P1; * K1, P1; rep from * across.

Row 3 (for girls):
K1, P1, K1, YO, K2 tog; P1, K1; * P1, K1; rep from * across.

Row 3 (for boys):
* K1, P1; rep from * to last 5 sts; K1, YO, K2 tog; P1, K1.

Row 4:
Rep Row 2.

Row 5:
K1; * P1, K1; rep from * across.

Row 6:
Rep Row 2.

Bind off in ribbing.

Finishing
Sew on buttons. Weave in all ends.

Saturday Stripe Socks

Stripe up the look of everyday socks in colors to please the guys and gals in your life. Cuffs can be worn up or down as the wearer desires. Shown on page 10 in two different color combinations

Sizes:
Note: Instructions are written for smaller size; changes for larger size are in parentheses.
Adult 9½" and 10½"

Materials:
Version One:
Worsted weight wool or wool-blend yarn, 2 oz **(132 yds, 52 g)** gray; 1 oz **(66 yds, 26 g)** each navy and red

Version Two:
Worsted weight wool or wool-blend yarn, 2 oz **(132 yds, 52 g)** variegated; 1 oz **(66 yds, 26 g)** each, blue and yellow
Size 6, 7" double-pointed knitting needles, or size required for gauge
Stitch holder
Size 18 tapestry needle

Gauge:
11 sts = 2" in stockinette stitch (knit one row, purl one row)

Instructions
Note: Change color by bringing new color under old color to prevent holes. Unless otherwise indicated, carry unused colors along joining.

Sock (make 2)
Note: Instructions are written for Version One colors. For Version Two, use variegated for gray, blue for navy and yellow for red.

With gray, cast on 44 **(48)** sts; divide by placing first 14 **(16)** sts on one needle, 16 sts on second needle, and 14 **(16)** sts on third needle; join, being careful not to twist sts **(see Special Techniques on page 6)**.

Note: Mark first st with contrasting color for beg of rnd.

Cuff:
Rnd 1 (right side):
* K1, P1; rep from * around.

Rep Rnd 1 until cuff measures 6". Join red.

Ankle:
Rnds 1 through 7:
Knit in following color sequence:

- ☐ red, 2 rnds
- ☐ navy, 2 rnds
- ☐ gray, 3 rnds

Rnds 8 through 14:
Rep Rnds 1 through 7. Cut all colors.

Heel:
Sl last 12 **(14)** sts of last rnd onto free needle; sl first 12 **(14)** sts of last rnd onto same needle; sl rem 20 sts onto a stitch holder for instep. With wrong side facing you, join navy.

Row 1 (wrong side):
Purl—24 **(28)** sts. Turn.

Row 2 (right side):
Sl 1 as to knit, knit rem sts. Turn.

Row 3:
Sl 1 as to purl, purl rem sts. Turn.

Row 4:
Rep Row 2.

Rep Rows 3 and 4 until heel measures about 2¼" **(2 ½")**, ending by working a right side row.

Turning Heel:
Row 1 (wrong side):
P15 **(17)**, P2 tog; P1. Turn, leaving rem sts unworked.

Row 2 (right side):
Sl 1 as to knit, K7 **(9)**, sl 1 as to knit, K1, PSSO; K1. Turn, leaving rem sts unworked.

Row 3:
Sl 1 as to purl, P8 **(10)**, P2 tog; P1. Turn, leaving rem sts unworked.

Row 4:
Sl 1 as to knit, K9 **(11)**, sl 1 as to knit, K1, PSSO; K1. Turn, leaving rem sts unworked.

Row 5:
Sl 1 as to purl, P10 **(12)**, P2 tog; P1. Turn, leaving rem sts unworked.

Row 6:
Sl 1 as to knit, K11 **(13)**, sl 1 as to knit, K1, PSSO; K1. Turn, leaving rem sts unworked.

continued

Saturday Stripe Socks *(continued)*

Row 7:
Sl 1 as to purl, P12 (14), P2 tog; P1. Turn.

Row 8:
Sl 1 as to knit, K13 (15), sl 1 as to knit, K1, PSSO; K1. Cut navy.

With right side facing you, slip last 8 (9) sts worked onto first needle, with red, knit these same 8 sts; on same needle pick up 11 (13) sts along left side of heel; on second needle, knit 20 sts from stitch holder; on third needle, pick up 11 (13) sts along right side of heel, knit rem 8 (9) sts of heel onto same needle—58 (64) sts.

Foot:
Rnd 1:
On first needle, knit to last 3 sts; K2 tog; K1; on second needle, K20; on third needle, K1, sl 1 as to knit, K1, PSSO; knit rem sts.

Rnd 2:
With navy, knit.

Rnd 3:
With navy, rep Rnd 1.

Rnd 4:
With gray, rep Rnd 2.

Rnds 5 and 6:
With gray, rep Rnds 1 and 2.

Rnds 7 through 14 (20):
Rep Rnds 1 and 2 in color sequence as established— 44 sts.

Knit each rnd in color sequence until foot measures 6½" (7") from picked up sts at heel. Cut gray and blue.

Toe Shaping:
Rnds 1 through 4:
With red, rep Rnds 1 and 2 of foot twice—40 sts.

Rnd 5:
On first needle, knit to last 3 sts; K2 tog; K1; on second needle, K1, sl 1 as to knit, K1, PSSO; knit to last 3 sts; K2 tog; K1; on third needle, K1, sl 1 as to knit, K1, PSSO; knit rem sts.

Rnd 6:
Knit.

Rnds 7 through 14:
Rep Rnds 5 and 6, 4 times—20 sts.

Knit sts from first needle onto third needle.

Finishing
With tapestry needle and red, weave toe together (see Special Techniques on page 6). Weave in all ends.

Snowtime Mittens

These cozy mittens are worked on four needles with contrasting stripes on the snug cuffs that keep out the cold.

Sizes:
Note: Instructions are written for size small; changes for larger sizes are in parentheses.

Small	Medium	Large
(2-4)	(6-8)	(10-12)

Materials:
Worsted weight brushed yarn, 2 (3, 4) oz [140 (210, 280) yds, 60 (90, 120) g] variegated purple; ½ oz (35 yds, 15 g) blue
Size 5, 7" double-pointed knitting needles, or size required for gauge
One 4" stitch holder
Markers
Size 16 tapestry needle

Gauge:
5 sts = 1" in stockinette stitch (knit one row, purl one row)
7 rows = 1"

Instructions

Mitten (make 2)
With variegated, cast on 30 (33, 39) sts; divide by placing 9 (12, 12) sts on first needle, 9 (12, 12) sts on second needle, and 12 (9, 15) sts on third needle; join, being careful not to twist stitches (see Special Techniques on page 6).

Note: Mark first st with contrasting color for beg of rnds.

Ribbing:
Rnd 1 (right side):
* K2, P1; rep from * around.

Rnds 2 through 6:
Rep Rnd 1.

Continue to rep Rnd 1 in following color sequence:

- ❏ blue, 2 rnds
- ❏ variegated, 2 rnds
- ❏ blue, 2 rnds
- ❏ variegated, 2 rnds

 blue, 2 rnds

 variegated, 2 rnds

Cut blue.

Hand:
Rnd 1:
With variegated, knit.

Rnds 2 through 5 (6, 7):
Rep Rnd 1.

Thumb Gusset:
Rnd 1:
K13 (15, 18), place marker on needle; inc (knit in front and back of next st); K1, inc; place marker on needle; knit rem sts—5 sts between markers for thumb.

Note: Slip markers on each rnd.

Rnds 2 and 3:
Knit.

Rnd 4:
Knit to first marker, sl marker, inc; knit to last st before marker, inc; sl marker, knit rem sts—7 thumb sts.

Rnds 5 and 6:
Knit.

Rnds 7 through 12 (15, 18):
Rep Rnds 4 through 6—11 (13, 15) thumb sts.

Dividing Rnd:
K13 (15, 18), remove marker; slip next 11 (13, 15) thumb sts onto a stitch holder, remove marker; cast on 2 (2, 3) sts (see **Figs 1** and **2**); knit rem sts—29 (32, 39) sts.

Continuing in rnds, knit even until piece measures 6" (7", 8") or ¹⁄₂" less than desired length.

Shaping:
Rnd 1:
K1 (0, 3); * K2 tog; K2; rep from * around—22 (24, 30) sts.

Rnd 2:
Knit.

Rnd 3:
K1 (0, 0); * K2 tog; K1; rep from * around—15 (16, 20) sts.

Rnd 4:
Rep Rnd 2.

Rnd 5:
K1 (0, 0); * K2 tog; rep from * around—8 (8, 10) sts.

Fig 1

Fig 2

Cut yarn, leaving an 8" end for sewing. Thread end into tapestry needle and weave through sts. Draw up tightly and weave in end securely.

Thumb:
With variegated, K11 (13, 15) sts from holder onto one needle; with second needle, pick up 1 st in each cast-on st at base of thumb; divide these 13 (15, 18) sts onto 3 needles.

Rnds 1 through 6 (8, 10):
Knit.

Thumb Shaping:
Rnd 1:
K1 (0, 0); * K2 tog, K1; rep from * around—9 (10, 12) sts.

Rnd 2:
K1 (0, 0); * K2 tog; rep from * around—5 (5, 6) sts.

Cut yarn, leaving a 6" end.

Finishing
Thread end into tapestry needle and weave through sts. Draw up tightly and weave in end securely. Weave in all ends.

So Sweet

These dear little booties will add the perfect endearing touch to baby's out-on-the-town wardrobe.

Size:
About 4" from heel to toe

Materials:
Baby weight yarn, 1/2 oz (85 yds, 15 g) each pink and white

Size 3 straight knitting needles, or size required for gauge

Size 7 straight knitting needles

Two 4" stitch holders

Size 18 tapestry needle

Two 3/8" buttons with shank

1/3 yd 3/8"-wide white lace

Sewing needle and matching thread

Gauge:
With smaller size needles,
    15 sts = 2" in garter stitch
    (knit every row)

Instructions

Bootie (make 2)

Starting at top with larger size needles and pink, cast on 41 sts.

Row 1 (right side):
P1; * yb, sl 1 as to purl, yf, P1; rep from * across.

Row 2:
Purl. Cut pink.

With white, rep Rows 1 and 2 until piece measures about 3", ending by working a Row 2.

Change to smaller size needles.

Ribbing:
Row 1 (right side):
K1; * P1, K1; rep from * across.

Row 2:
P1; * K1, P1; rep from * across.

Row 3:
K1; * YO, K2 tog; rep from * across.

Row 4:
Rep Row 2. At end of row—41 sts.

Instep:
Row 1 (right side):
* K1, P1; rep from * 13 times more; sl rem 13 sts onto a stitch holder.

Row 2:
K1; * P1, K1; rep from * 6 times more; sl rem 13 sts onto a stitch holder.

Row 3:
P1; * K1, P1; rep from * 6 times more.

Row 4:
K1; * P1, K1; rep from * 6 times more.

Rep Rows 3 and 4 until instep measures 1 3/4" long, ending by working a Row 4.

Cut yarn, leaving sts on needle.

Foot:
With right side facing you and instep at top, with pink, knit across 13 sts on first holder, pick up 14 sts along side edge of instep, knit across 15 instep sts, pick up 14 sts along other side of instep; slip 13 sts from holder onto free needle and knit these sts—69 sts.

Rows 1 through 11:
Knit.

Sole:
Row 1 (right side):
K5, K2 tog; K20, K2 tog; K11, K2 tog; K20, K2 tog; K5—65 sts.

Rows 2, 4, 6, and 8:
Knit.

Row 3:
K4, K2 tog; K20, K2 tog; K9, K2 tog; K20, K2 tog; K4—61 sts.

Row 5:
K3, K2 tog; K20, K2 tog; K7, K2 tog; K20, K2 tog; K3—57 sts.

Row 7:
K2, K2 tog; K20, K2 tog; K5, K2 tog; K20, K2 tog; K2—53 sts.

Row 9:
K1, K2 tog; K20, K2 tog; K3, K2 tog; K20, K2 tog; K1—49 sts.

Bind off all sts.

Cut yarn, leaving an 8" end for sewing.

With tapestry needle, sew bottom and back seam.

Ankle Strap (make 2)

With smaller size needles and pink, cast on 45 sts.

Bind off all sts.

Finishing
Step 1:

Referring to photo for placement, place one strap around ankle of each bootie, overlapping ends at center front. Sew button through both thicknesses of overlapped ends of each strap. Tack straps in place.

Step 2:

Sew lace around edge of each instep.

Spirited Stripes

designed by Sandy Scoville

Even beginning knitters can easily create this striking tunic sweater. Choose your favorite worsted weight colors and knit away!

Sizing:

Note: Instructions are written for size small; changes for larger sizes are in parentheses.

Size:	Small	Medium	Large
Chest Measurement:	30"-32"	34"-36"	38"-40"
Finished Chest Measurement:	38"	42"	46"
Length from shoulder seam:	29"	30"	31"

Materials:

Worsted weight yarn, 6 (7, 8) oz [420 (490, 560) yds, 200 (230, 265) g] each, aqua, green, orange, pink, and rose
Size 7, 29" circular knitting needle, or size required for gauge
Size 7, 16" circular knitting needle (for collar)
Size 7, 10" double-pointed knitting needles (for sleeve)
Markers
One 6" stitch holder
Size 16 tapestry needle

Gauge:

9 sts = 2" in stockinette stitch (knit one row, purl one row)
6 rows = 1"

Instructions

Body

Note: Body is worked in rnds.

With 29" circular needle and aqua, cast on 172 (190, 206) sts.

Note: Beg rnd in first cast-on st.
Rnd 1 (right side):
Knit.

Rep Rnd 1 in following color sequence:

❑ aqua, 22 rnds

❑ green, 1 rnd

❑ aqua, 3 rnds

❑ green, 1 rnd

❑ aqua, 2 rnds

continued

65

Spirited Stripes *(continued)*

- ☐ green, 1 rnd
- ☐ aqua, 1 rnd
- ☐ green, 1 rnd
- ☐ aqua, 1 rnd
- ☐ green, 1 rnd
- ☐ aqua, 1 rnd
- ☐ green, 2 rnds
- ☐ aqua, 1 rnd
- ☐ green, 3 rnds
- ☐ aqua, 1 rnd
- ☐ green, 22 rnds
- ☐ orange, 1 rnd
- ☐ green, 3 rnds
- ☐ orange, 1 rnd
- ☐ green, 2 rnds
- ☐ orange, 1 rnd
- ☐ green, 1 rnd
- ☐ orange, 1 rnd
- ☐ green, 1 rnd
- ☐ orange, 1 rnd
- ☐ green, 1 rnd

- ☐ orange, 2 rnds
- ☐ green, 1 rnd
- ☐ orange, 3 rnds
- ☐ green, 1 rnd
- ☐ orange, 22 rnds
- ☐ pink, 1 rnd
- ☐ orange, 3 rnds
- ☐ pink, 1 rnd
- ☐ orange, 2 rnds
- ☐ pink, 1 rnd
- ☐ orange, 1 rnd
- ☐ pink, 1 rnd
- ☐ orange, 1 rnd
- ☐ pink, 1 rnd
- ☐ orange, 1 rnd
- ☐ pink, 2 rnds
- ☐ orange, 1 rnd
- ☐ pink, 3 rnds
- ☐ orange, 1 rnd
- ☐ pink, 2 (2, 8) rnds

Your piece should measure about 21" (21", 22"). Continuing with pink, K86 (95, 103) for upper front. Turn, leaving rem 86 (95, 103) sts on needle for back. Mark front and back for underarm.

Upper Front:

Row 1 (wrong side):
Purl.

Row 2 (right side):
Knit.

Row 3:
Purl.

Rep Rows 2 and 3 in following color sequence:

- ☐ pink, 16 (16, 10) rows
- ☐ rose, 1 row
- ☐ pink, 3 rows
- ☐ rose, 1 row
- ☐ pink, 2 rows
- ☐ rose, 1 row
- ☐ pink, 1 row
- ☐ rose, 1 row

- ☐ pink, 1 row
- ☐ rose, 1 row
- ☐ pink, 1 row
- ☐ rose, 2 rows
- ☐ pink, 1 row
- ☐ rose, 3 rows
- ☐ pink, 1 row
- ☐ rose, 4 (6, 8) rows

Neckline and Shoulder Shaping:

Row 1 (right side):
With rose, K30 (32, 36) for left front shoulder; join new skein of yarn, K26 (31, 31) for neckline; slip neckline sts onto a stitch holder; K30 (32, 36) for right front shoulder.

Row 2:
Purl.

Row 3:
K28 (30, 34), K2 tog; on right front shoulder, sl 1 as to knit, K1, PSSO; K28 (30, 34).

Row 4:
Purl.

Row 5:
K27 (29, 33), K2 tog; on right front shoulder, sl 1 as to knit, K1, PSSO; K27 (29, 33).

Row 6:
Purl.

Row 7:
K26 (28, 32), K2 tog; on right front shoulder, sl 1 as to knit, K1, PSSO; K26 (28, 32).

Row 8:
Purl.

Bind off all sts.

Upper Back:

Hold back with wrong side facing you; join pink and work same as for upper front to neckline and shoulder shaping.

With rose, rep Rows 2 and 3 only of upper front 4 times.

Bind off all sts.

Sleeve (make 2)

With double-pointed needles and aqua, cast on 40 (46, 46) sts; divide onto 3 needles.

Note: Sleeve is worked in rnds; mark beg of rnds. Beg rnd in first cast on st (see Special Techniques on page 6).

Rnds 1 through 5:
Knit.

Rnd 6:
K1, inc (knit in front and back of next st); knit to last 2 sts; inc; K1.

Keeping to color sequence of body, rep Rnds 1 through 6 until there are 76 (82, 84) sts on needle and sleeve measures about 19" (19", 20").

Bind off all sts.

Sew shoulder seams, leaving 9" open on front and back for center neck opening.

Collar

Note: Collar is worked in rnds; mark beg of rnds. Beg rnd in first cast-on st.

Hold sweater with right side facing you and shoulders at top. With 16" circular needle and rose, and beg on front at left shoulder seam, pick up 8 sts along left neck edge, knit 26 (31, 31) neckline sts from holder, pick up 8 sts along right neck edge, pick up 32 sts across back—74 (79, 79) sts.

Rows 1 through 8:
Knit.

Bind off all sts. Collar will roll to right side.

Finishing

Hold right sides of sleeves and body together; with pink, matching center of last row of sleeves to shoulder seams, sew sleeves to body.

Sporty Cuffed Socks

designed by Sandy Scoville

Knit these fun-to-wear socks in the favorite team or school colors and they'll wear them at outdoor winter sporting events—or, more probably, in front of the television.

Size:

Note: Instructions are written for smaller size; changes for larger size are in parentheses.
Adult 9½" and 10½"

Materials:

Worsted weight yarn, 2 oz (140 yds, 60 g) white fleck; 1 oz (70 yds, 30 g) each, red fleck and blue fleck
Size 6, 7" double-pointed knitting needles, or size required for gauge
Stitch holder
Size 16 tapestry needle

Gauge:

11 sts = 2" in stockinette stitch (knit one row, purl one row)

Instructions

Note: Change color by bringing new color under old color to prevent holes. Unless otherwise indicated, carry unused colors along joining.

Sock (make 2)

Cuff:
With white, cast on 44 (48) sts; divide by placing first 14 (16) sts on one needle, 16 sts on second needle, and 14 (16) sts on third needle; join, being careful not to twist sts (see Special Techniques on page 6).

Note: Mark first st with contrasting color for beg of rnd.

Rnd 1 (right side of sock, wrong side of cuff):
* K1, P1; rep from * around.

Rnd 2:
Rep Rnd 1. Cut white.

Rnds 3 through 5:
With blue, purl.

continued

Spirited Stripes *(continued)*

Rnd 6:
With red, purl.

Rnds 7 through 11:
With red, rep Rnd 1.

Rnds 12 through 20:
Rep Rnds 3 through 11.

Rnds 21 through 23:
Rep Rnds 3 through 5. Cut blue and red.

Rnd 24:
With white, purl.

Ankle:
Rep Rnd 1 until sock measures 7½". Cut white.

Heel:
Slip last 12 (14) sts of last rnd onto free needle; slip first 12 (14) sts of last rnd onto same needle; slip remaining 20 sts onto a stitch holder for instep.

With wrong side facing you, join red in first st.

Row 1 (wrong side):
Sl 1 as to purl; purl rem sts. Turn.

Row 2 (right side):
Sl 1 as to knit; knit rem sts. Turn.

Rep Rows 1 and 2 until heel measures 2¼" (2½"), ending by working a Row 2.

Turning Heel:
Row 1 (wrong side):
P15 (17), P2 tog; P1. Turn, leaving rem sts unworked.

Row 2 (right side):
Sl 1 as to knit, K7 (9), sl 1 as to knit, K1, PSSO; K1. Turn, leaving rem sts unworked.

Row 3:
Sl 1 as to purl, P8 (10), P2 tog; P1. Turn, leaving rem sts unworked.

Row 4:
Sl 1 as to knit, K9 (11), sl 1 as to knit, K1, PSSO; K1. Turn, leaving rem sts unworked.

Row 5:
Sl 1 as to purl, P10 (12), P2 tog; P1. Turn, leaving rem sts unworked.

Row 6:
Sl 1 as to knit, K11 (13), sl 1 as to knit, K1, PSSO; K1. Turn, leaving rem sts unworked.

Row 7:
Sl 1 as to purl, P12 (14), P2 tog; P1. Turn, leaving rem sts unworked.

Row 8:
Sl 1 as to knit, K13 (15), sl 1 as to knit, K1, PSSO; K1. Cut red.

With right side of heel facing you, on free needle, with white, pick up 11 (13) sts along left side of heel; on second needle, knit 20 sts from stitch holder; on third needle, pick up 11 (13) sts along right side of heel; knit first 8 (10) sts of heel onto same needle; slip rem 8 (10) red sts of heel onto beg of first needle—58 (62) sts.

Foot:
Rnd 1:
On first needle, with white, knit to last 3 sts; K2 tog; K1; on second needle, K20; on third needle, K1, sl 1 as to knit, K1, PSSO; knit rem sts.

Rnd 2:
Knit.

Rnds 3 through 14 (20):
Rep Rnds 1 and 2 six (nine) times—44 sts.

Knit even until foot measures 6½" (7") from picked up sts at heel. Join red; cut white.

Toe Shaping:
Rnds 1 through 4:
Rep Rnds 1 and 2 of foot twice—40 sts.

Rnd 5:
On first needle, knit to last 3 sts; K2 tog; K1; on second needle, K1, sl 1 as to knit, K1, PSSO; knit to last 3 sts; K2 tog; K1; on third needle, K1, sl 1 as to knit, K1, PSSO; knit rem sts.

Rnd 6:
Knit.

Rnds 7 through 14:
Rep Rnds 5 and 6, four times—20 sts.

Knit sts from first needle onto third needle.

Cut yarn, leaving a 20" end for weaving.

Finishing
With tapestry needle and red, weave toe together (see Special Techniques on page 6). Weave in all ends.

Winter Day Knee Socks

Choose colors as wild or as subdued as the wearer desires and be ready for even the coldest weather.

Size:
One size (about 13" above heel to knee)

Materials:
Worsted weight yarn, 6 oz (420 yds, 180 g) white fleck;
3 oz (210 yds, 90 g) blue
Size 6, 7" double-pointed knitting needles, or size required for gauge
Stitch holder
Size 16 tapestry needle

Gauge:
5 sts = 1" in stockinette stitch (knit one row, purl one row)

Instructions
Note: Change color by bringing new color under old color to prevent holes. Unless otherwise indicated, carry unused colors along joining.

Sock (make 2)
With white, cast on 40 sts; divide by placing first 14 sts on one needle, 14 sts on second needle, and 12 sts on third needle; join, being careful not to twist sts (see Special Techniques on page 6).

Ribbing:
Rnd 1:
* K1, P1; rep from * around.

Rep Rnd 1 until ribbing measures 1½".

Calf:
Rnds 1 through 9:
With white, knit.

Rnd 10:
With blue, knit.

Rnds 11 through 13:
Purl.

Rnds 14 through 39:
Rep Rnds 1 through 13 twice.

Rnds 40 through 48:
With white, knit.

Rnd 49:
With blue, K8, K2 tog; rep from * around—36 sts.

Rnds 50 through 52:
With blue, purl.

Rnds 53 through 78:
Rep Rnds 1 through 13 twice.

Note: Remainder of sock is worked with white only. Cut blue.

Rnds 79 through 85:
Knit.

Heel:
Divide sts by placing 18 sts on first needle for heel, slip remaining 18 sts onto a stitch holder for instep.

Work back and forth on 18 heel sts only as follows:

Row 1:
* K1, sl l as to purl; rep from * 8 times more.

Row 2:
Purl.

Rep Rows 1 and 2 until heel measures 2".

Next Row:
Rep Row 1.

Turning Heel:
Row 1 (wrong side):
P11, P2 tog; P1. Turn, leaving rem sts unworked.

Row 2 (right side):
Sl 1 as to purl, K5, sl 1 as to knit, K1, PSSO; K1. Turn, leaving rem sts unworked.

Row 3:
Sl 1 as to purl, P6, P2 tog; P1. Turn, leaving rem sts unworked.

Row 4:
Sl 1 as to purl, K7, sl 1 as to knit, K1, PSSO; K1. Turn, leaving rem sts unworked.

Row 5:
Sl 1 as to purl, P8, P2 tog; P1. Turn, leaving rem sts unworked.

Row 6:
Sl 1 as to purl, K9, sl 1 as to knit, K1, PSSO; K1—12 sts.

continued

Foot:
Rnd 1:
Using needle with 12 heel sts, pick up 9 sts along left side of heel; with free needle, knit sts from holder; with free needle, pick up 9 sts along right side of heel; K6 from first needle—15 sts on first needle, 18 sts on second needle, and 15 sts on third needle.

Rnd 2:
Knit to last 3 sts on first needle; K2 tog; K1; knit across sts on second needle; on third needle, K1, sl 1 as to knit, K1, PSSO; knit rem sts—46 sts.

Rnd 3:
Knit.

Rep Rnds 2 and 3 five times—36 sts. Knit even until foot measures 2" less than desired length.

Toe Shaping:
Rnd 1:
On first needle, knit to last 3 sts; K2 tog; K1; on second needle, sl 1 as to knit, K1, PSSO; knit to last 3 sts; K2 tog; K1; on third needle, sl 1 as to knit, K1, PSSO; knit rem sts—32 sts.

Rnd 2:
Knit.

Rep Rnds 1 and 2 five times—12 sts.

Next Rnd:
On first needle, K3, slip these sts onto third needle. Cut yarn, leaving a 20" end for weaving.

Finishing
With tapestry needle and yarn end, weave sts together (See Special Techniques on page 6). Weave in all ends.

What A Hoot! Baby Sweater

The yoke of this cute sweater is fashioned with cables that form a clever trio of owls. Sew on buttons for a wide-eyed, whimsical touch.

Sizing:
Note: Instructions are written for smaller size; changes for other size are in parentheses.

Size: Small   **Medium**
   (1-2)   (3-4)

Materials:
Worsted weight yarn, 5 **(6)** oz **[**350 **(420)** yds, 150 **(180)** g**]** yellow

Size 8 straight knitting needles, or size required for gauge
Size 6 straight knitting needles
Two 4" stitch holders
Cable needle
Size 16 tapestry needle
Six ³/₈"-diameter brown buttons
Sewing needle and black thread

Gauge:
With larger size needles, 9 sts = 2" in stockinette stitch (knit one row, purl one row)
6 rows = 1"

Pattern Stitch
Cable Twist (worked over 8 sts):
Sl next 2 sts to cable needle and hold in back of work; K2, knit 2 sts from cable needle; sl next 2 sts onto cable needle and hold in front of work; K2, knit 2 sts from cable needle—cable twist made.

Instructions

Back

Ribbing:
With smaller size needles, cast on 51 **(55)** sts.

Row 1 (right side):
K1; ***** P1, K1; rep from ***** across.

Row 2:
P1; ***** K1, P1; rep from ***** across.

Rep Rows 1 and 2 until ribbing measures 1¹/₂", ending by working a Row 2.

Change to larger size needles.

Body:
Work even in stock st until piece measures 8" **(9¹/₂")**, ending by working a purl row.

Armhole Shaping:
Row 1 (right side):
Bind off 2 sts; knit rem sts.

Row 2:
Bind off 2 sts; purl rem sts—47 **(51)** sts.

Row 3:
K2 tog; knit to last 2 sts; sl 1 as to knit, K1, PSSO.

Row 4:
Purl.

Rows 5 and 6:
Rep Rows 3 and 4—43 **(47)** sts.

Work even until armhole measures 4" **(4³/₄")**, ending by working a purl row.

Rep Rows 1 and 2 until ribbing measures 1½", ending by working a Row 1.

Next Row:
Rep Row 2, inc one st at end of last row—52 (56) sts.

Change to larger size needles.

Body:
Work even in stock st until piece measures 1" less than back to armhole shaping, ending by working a purl row.

Owl Yoke:
Row 1 (right side):
K19 (20), P14 (16), K19 (20).

Row 2:
Purl.

Rows 3 and 4:
Rep Rows 1 and 2.

Row 5 (cable twist row):
K19 (20), P3 (4), work cable twist (see Pattern Stitch) over next 8 sts; P3 (4), K19 (20).

Row 6:
P19 (20), K3 (4), P8, K3 (4), P19 (20).

Armhole Shaping:
Row 1:
Bind off 2 sts; K2, P18 (20), K8, P18 (20), K4.

Row 2:
Bind off 2 sts; P17 (18), K3 (4), P8, K3 (4), P17 (18)—48 (52) sts.

Row 3:
K2 tog; P18 (20), K8, P18 (20), sl 1 as to knit, K1, PSSO—46 (50) sts.

Row 4:
P16 (17), K3 (4), P8, K3 (4); purl rem sts.

Row 5 (cable twist row):
P2 tog; P3, cable twist over next 8 sts; P6 (8), K8, P6 (8), cable twist over next 8 sts; P3, sl 1 as to purl, P1, PSSO—44 (48) sts.

Row 6:
K4, P8, K6 (8), P8, K6 (8), P8, K4.

Row 7:
P4, K8, P6 (8), K8, P6 (8), K8, P4.

Row 8:
Rep Row 6.

Neck and Shoulder Shaping:
Row 1:
Bind off 4 sts; K 9 (10) sts for right shoulder; slip next 17 (19) sts onto a stitch holder for back of neck; join new skein of yarn and knit across rem 13 sts for left shoulder.

Note: Continue to work each shoulder with a separate skein of yarn.

Row 2:
Bind off 4 sts; purl across sts of left shoulder to last 2 sts at neck edge; P2 tog; P2 tog at neck edge of right shoulder; purl rem sts.

Row 3:
Bind off 4 sts; knit across.

Row 4:
Rep Row 2.

Row 5:
Bind off rem 3 (4) sts of right shoulder; knit rem sts of left shoulder.

Bind off rem 3 (4) sts.

Front

Ribbing:
With smaller size needles, cast on 51 (55) sts.

Row 1 (right side):
K1; * P1, K1; rep from * across.

Row 2:
P1; * K1, P1; rep from * across.

continued

Row 9 (cable twist row):
P4, K8, P6 (8), cable twist over next 8 sts; P6 (8), K8, P4.

Rows 10 through 13:
Rep Rows 6 and 7 twice.

Row 14:
Rep Row 6.

Row 15 (cable twist row):
P4; * cable twist over next 8 sts; P6 (8); rep from * once more; cable twist over next 8 sts; P4.

Row 16:
K4, P8, K20 (24), P8, K4.

Row 17:
P4, K8, P20 (24), K8, P4.

Rows 18 and 19:
Rep Rows 16 and 17.

Row 20:
Rep Row 16.

Row 21 (cable twist row):
P4, cable twist over next 8 sts; P20 (24), cable twist over next 8 sts; P4.

Row 22:
Knit.

Size Small Only:
Continue with Neck and Shoulder Shaping below.

Size Medium Only:
Row 23:
Purl.

Row 24:
Knit.

Rows 25 and 26:
Rep Rows 23 and 24.

Continue with Neck and Shoulder Shaping below.

Neck and Shoulder Shaping:
Row 1:
P14 (15) for left shoulder; slip next 16 (18) sts onto a stitch holder for front of neck; join new skein of yarn, P14 (15) for right shoulder.

Note: Continue to work each shoulder with a separate skein of yarn.

Row 2:
Knit across sts of right shoulder to last 2 sts at neck edge; K2 tog; at left neck edge, sl 1 as to knit, K1, PSSO; knit rem sts of left shoulder.

Row 3:
Purl across sts of each shoulder.

Rows 4 and 5:
Rep Rows 2 and 3.

Row 6:
Rep Row 2.

Row 7:
Bind off 4 sts; purl rem sts.

Row 8:
Bind off 4 sts; knit rem sts.

Rows 9 and 10:
Rep Rows 7 and 8.

Row 11:
Bind off rem 3 (4) sts of left shoulder; purl rem sts.

Bind off rem 3 (4) sts.

Sleeve (make 2)
Ribbing:
With smaller size needles, cast on 29 (33) sts.

Row 1 (right side):
K1; * P1, K1; rep from * across.

Row 2:
P1; * K1, P1; rep from * across.

Rep Rows 1 and 2 until piece measures 2½" (3"), ending by working a Row 2.

Change to larger size needles.

Body:
Row 1:
Knit.

Row 2:
Purl.

Rows 3 through 8:
Rep Rows 1 and 2 three times.

Row 9:
Inc (knit in front and back of next st); knit to last st; inc.

Rows 10 through 33:
Rep Rows 2 through 9 three times more—37 (41) sts.

Work even in stock st until sleeve measures 9½" (10½"), ending by working a purl row.

Cap Shaping:
Row 1:
Bind off 2 sts; knit across.

Row 2:
Bind off 2 sts; purl across—33 (37) sts.

Row 3:
K2 tog; knit to last 2 sts; sl 1 as to knit, K1, PSSO.

Row 4:
Purl.

Rows 5 through 10:
Rep Rows 3 and 4 three times—25 (29) sts.

Row 11:
K2 tog; knit to last 2 sts; sl 1 as to knit, K1, PSSO.

Row 12:
P2 tog; purl to last 2 sts; sl 1 as to purl, P1, PSSO.

Rows 13 through 18 (20):
Rep Rows 11 and 12 three (four) times—9 sts.

Bind off all sts.

Sew right shoulder seam.

Neck Ribbing:
With right side facing you and with smaller size needles, beg at left front neck edge, pick up 10 sts along left front neck edge, slip sts from front holder onto free needle and knit onto needle, pick up 10 sts along right front neck edge to shoulder seam; pick up 5 sts along right back neck edge; slip sts from back holder onto free needle and knit onto needle; pick up 5 sts along left back neck edge—63 (67) sts.

Row 1:
K1; * P1, K1; rep from * across.

Row 2:
P1; * K1, P1; rep from * across.

Rep Rows 1 and 2 until ribbing measures $^3/_4$".

Bind off in ribbing.

Finishing
Sew left shoulder seam and neck ribbing. Sew sleeves to body, matching center of last row of sleeves to shoulder seams. Sew side and sleeve seams. Weave in all ends. Referring to photo for placement, sew buttons in place for eyes.

Winter Warmth

Count on this hat and scarf set to lift the spirits and to look your best even on the most blustery days.

Size:
Hat: one size
Scarf: 6" x 60"

Materials:
Mohair type worsted weight yarn, *for hat*, 1 oz (90 yds, 30 g) red; *for scarf*, 2 oz (180 yds, 60 g) red
Size 10, 14" straight knitting needles, or size required for gauge
Size 9, 14" straight knitting needles
Size 16 tapestry needle

Gauge:
With larger size needles, 7 sts = 2" in K1, P1 ribbing

Pattern Stitch
Row 1 (right side):
K1, wrap yarn twice around needle , P1 **(Fig 1)**; * wrap yarn twice around needle, K1 **(Fig 2)**, wrap yarn twice around needle, P1; rep from * across.

Row 2:
K1, drop both wraps, P1; * drop both wraps, K1; drop both wraps, P1; rep from * across.

Row 3:
* K1, P1; rep from * across.

Rows 4 through 6:
Rep Row 3.

Rep Rows 1 through 6 for patt.

Instructions

Hat

Ribbing:
With smaller size needles, cast on 90 sts.

Row 1 (right side):
* K1, P1; rep from * across.

Rows 2 through 4:
Rep Row 1.

continued

Winter Warmth *(continued)*

Change to larger size needles.

Body:
Rows 1 through 24:
Rep Rows 1 through 6 of Pattern Stitch (on page 73) four times.

Top Shaping:
Row 1:
K3 tog; P1, K1, P1; * K3 tog; P1, (K1, P1) twice; rep from * 9 times more; K3 tog; P1—66 sts.

Row 2:
* K1, P1; rep from * across.

Row 3:
* K3 tog; P1, K1, P1; rep from * across—44 sts.

Row 4:
Rep Row 2.

Row 5:
K1, P1; * K3 tog; P1; rep from * 9 times more; K1, P1—24 sts.

Row 6:
Rep Row 2.

Finishing
Cut yarn, leaving a 24" end. Thread end into tapestry needle and weave through all sts. Draw up tightly and fasten securely. Sew side seam, carefully matching rows of long sts. Weave in ends.

Scarf

Ribbing:
With smaller size needles, cast on 28 sts.

Row 1 (right side):
* K1, P1; rep from * across.

Rows 2 through 4:
Rep Row 1.

Change to larger size needles.

Body:
Rep Rows 1 through 6 of Pattern Stitch (on page 73) until piece meaures 60", ending by working a Row 2.

Change to smaller size needles.

Ribbing:
Row 1 (right side):
* K1, P1; rep from * across.

Rows 2 and 3:
Rep Row 1.

Bind off in ribbing.

Weave in ends.

Young Fisherman Set

designed by Sandy Scoville

Boys and girls alike will love having a knit hat and sweater an experienced knitter has made just for them.

Sizing:
Note: Instructions are written for size small; changes for larger sizes are in parentheses.

Sweater Size:	Small (4-6)	Medium (8-10)	Large (12-14)
Chest Measurement:	24"	28"	32"
Finished Chest Measurement:	28"	32"	36"
Length:	16"	17"	18"
Sleeve Length:	11"	13"	15"

Hat:
One size

Materials:

Worsted weight yarn, *for sweater*, 7 (8, 9) oz [490 (560, 630) yds, 200 (228, 252) g] off white; *for hat*, 3½ oz (240 yds, 100 g) off white

Size 8 straight knitting needles, or size required for gauge

Size 6 straight knitting needles (for sweater)

Cable needle

Markers

Three 4" stitch holders

Six ⅝"-diameter wooden buttons

Size 16 tapestry needle

Sewing needle and matching thread

Gauge:

With larger size needles, 5 sts = 1" in stockinette stitch (knit one row, purl one row)

6 rows = 1"

Pattern Stitches

Cable Back (CB):
Sl next 2 sts onto cable needle, hold in back of work, K2, K2 from cable needle—CB made.

Cable Front (CF):
Sl next 2 sts onto cable needle, hold in front of work, K2, K2 from cable needle—CF made.

Sweater Instructions

Right Front

Ribbing:
With larger size needles, cast on 36 (42, 48) sts. Change to smaller size needles.

Row 1 (right side):
* K1, P1; rep from * across.

Row 2:
* P1, K1; rep from * across.

Rows 3 through 6:
Rep Rows 1 and 2 twice.

Change to larger size needles.

Body:
Note: Markers are used to separate pattern stitches. They are set in place on the first row, and should be moved from the left-hand needle to the right-hand needle as you come to them. They may be removed when you are familiar with the pattern.

Row 1 (right side):
(K4, P2) 2 (3, 3) times; place marker; P2, K8, P2; place marker; (K4, P2) 2 (2, 3) times.

Row 2:
(K2, P4) 2 (2, 3) times; K2, P8, K2, (K2, P4) 2 (3, 3) times.

Row 3:
(K4, P2) 2 (3, 3) times; P2, CB (see Pattern Stitches); CF (see Pattern Stitches); P2, (K4, P2) 2 (2, 3) times.

Row 4:
Rep Row 2.

Row 5:
K2, (P2, K4) 1 (2, 2) times; P2, K2, P2, K8, P2, K2, (P2, K4) 1 (1, 2) times; P2, K2.

Row 6:
P2, (K2, P4) 1 (1, 2) times; K2, P2, K2, P8, K2, P2, (K2, P4) 1 (2, 2) times; K2, P2.

Row 7:
K2, (P2, K4) 1 (2, 2) times; P2, K2, P2, CF; CB; P2, K2, (P2, K4) 1 (1, 2) times; P2, K2.

Row 8:
Rep Row 6.

Row 9:
(P2, K4) 2 (3, 3) times; P2, K8, P2, (P2, K4) 2 (2, 3) times.

Row 10:
(P4, K2) 2 (2, 3) times; K2, P8, K2, (P4, K2) 2 (3, 3) times.

Row 11:
(P2, K4) 2 (3, 3) times; P2, CB; CF; P2, (P2, K4) 2 (2, 3) times.

Row 12:
Rep Row 10.

Row 13:
(K4, P2) 2 (3, 3) times; P2, K8, P2, (K4, P2) 2 (2, 3) times.

Row 14:
Rep Row 2.

Row 15:
(K4, P2) 2 (3, 3) times; P2, CF; CB; P2, (K4, P2) 2 (3, 3) times.

Row 16:
Rep Row 2.

Rows 17 and 18:
Rep Rows 5 and 6.

Row 19:
K2, (P2, K4) 1 (2, 2) times; P2, K2, P2, CB; CF; P2, K2, (P2, K4) 1 (2, 2) times; P2, K2.

Row 20:
Rep Row 6.

Rows 21 and 22:
Rep Rows 9 and 10.

continued

Row 23:
(P2, K4) 2 (3, 3) times; P2, CF; CB; P2, (P2, K4) 2 (2, 3) times.

Row 24:
Rep Row 10.

Rep Rows 1 through 24 twice.

Rep Rows 1 through 4 (8, 12).

Neckline Shaping:
Row 1:
Bind off 6 sts; work in patt across.

Row 2:
Work in patt across.

Row 3:
Sl 1 as to knit, K1, PSSO; work in patt across.

Row 4:
Work in patt across.

Continuing to work in patt, rep Rows 3 an 4 until 24 (28, 32) sts rem on needle, ending by working a Row 4.

Work even in patt for 10 rows.

Bind off all sts.

Buttonhole Placket:
Note: Buttonholes are worked on right front for girls. For boys, reverse instructions for right and left plackets.

With right side facing you and with larger size needles, pick up 42 (48, 52) sts along center front opening.

Row 1 (wrong side):
* P1, K1; rep from * across.

Row 2 (right side):
* K1, P1; rep from * across.

Size Small Only:
Row 3:
P1, K1, P1, bind off 2 sts; * (K1, P1) twice; K1, bind off 2 sts; (P1, K1) twice; P1, bind off 2 sts; rep from * once more; (K1, P1) twice; K1, bind off 2 sts; P1, K1.

Row 4:
K1, P1, cast on 2 sts; * (K1, P1) twice; K1, cast on 2 sts; (P1, K1) twice; P1, cast on 2 sts; rep from * once more; (K1, P1) twice; K1, cast on 2 sts; P1, K1, P1.

Size Medium Only:
Row 3:
P1, K1, P1, bind off 2 sts; * (K1, P1) twice; K1, bind off 2 sts; (P1, K1) twice; P1, bind off 2 sts; rep from * twice more; P1, K1, P1.

Row 4:
P1, K1, P1, cast on 2 sts; * (K1, P1) twice; K1, cast on 2 sts; (P1, K1) twice; P1, cast on 2 sts; rep from * twice more; P1, K1, P1.

Size Large Only:
Row 3:
P1, K1, P1, bind off 2 sts; * (K1, P1) twice; K1, bind off 2 sts; (P1, K1) twice; P1, bind off 2 sts; rep from * twice more; (K1, P1) twice; K1.

Row 4:
(K1, P1) twice; K1, cast on 2 sts; * (P1, K1) twice; P1, cast on 2 sts; (P1, K1) twice; P1, cast on 2 sts; rep from * twice more; P1, K1, P1.

All Sizes:
Row 5:
* P1, K1; rep from * across.

Bind off all sts in patt.

Left Front
Ribbing:
With larger size needles, cast on 36 (42, 48) sts. Change to smaller size needles.

Row 1 (right side):
* K1, P1; rep from * across.

Row 2:
* P1, K1; rep from * across.

Rows 3 through 6:
Rep Rows 1 and 2 twice.

Change to larger size needles.

Body:
Row 1:
(K4, P2) 2 (2, 3) times; place marker; P2, K8, P2; place marker; (K4, P2) 2 (3, 3) times.

Row 2:
(K2, P4) 2 (3, 3) times; K2, P8, K2, (K2, P4) 2 (2, 3) times.

Row 3:
(K4, P2) 2 (2, 3) times; P2, CB; CF; P2, (K4, P2) 2 (3, 3) times.

Row 4:
Rep Row 2.

Row 5:
K2, (P2, K4) 1 (1, 2) times; P2, K2, P2, K8, P2, K2, (P2, K4) 1 (2, 2) times; P2, K2.

Row 6:
P2, (K2, P4) 1 (2, 2) times; K2, P2, K2, P8, K2, P2, (K2, P4) 1 (1, 2) times; K2, P2.

Row 7:
K2, (P2, K4) 1 (1, 2) times; P2, K2, P2, CF; CB; P2, K2, (P2, K4) 1 (2, 2) times; P2, K2.

Row 8:
Rep Row 6.

Row 9:
(P2, K4) 2 (2, 3) times; P2, K8, P2, (P2, K4) 2 (3, 3) times.

Row 10:
(P4, K2) 2 (3, 3) times; K2, P8, K2, (P4, K2) 2 (2, 3) times.

Row 11:
(P2, K4) 2 (2, 3) times P2, CB; CF; P2, (P2, K4) 2 (3, 3) times.

Row 12:
Rep Row 10.

Row 13:
(K4, P2) 2 (2, 3) times; P2, K8, P2, (K4, P2) 2 (3, 3) times.

Row 14:
Rep Row 2.

Row 15:
(K4, P2) 2 (2, 3) times; P2, CF; CB; P2, (K4, P2) 2 (3, 3) times.

Row 16:
Rep Row 2.

Rows 17 and 18:
Rep Rows 5 and 6.

Row 19:
K2, (P2, K4) 1 (1, 2) times; P2, K2, P2, CB; CF; P2, K2, (P2, K4) 1 (2, 2) times; P2, K2.

Row 20:
Rep Row 6.

Rows 21 and 22:
Rep Rows 9 and 10.

Row 23:
(P2, K4) 2 (2, 3) times; P2, CF; CB; P2, (P2, K4) two (3, 3) times.

Row 24:
Rep Row 10.

Rep Rows 1 through 24 twice.

Rep Rows 1 through 4 (8, 12).

Neckline Shaping:
Row 1:
Work in patt across.

Row 2:
Bind off 6 sts; work in patt across.

Row 3:
Work in patt to last 2 sts; K2 tog.

Row 4:
Work in patt across.

Continuing to work in patt, rep Rows 3 and 4 until 24 (28, 32) sts rem on needle, ending by working a Row 4.

Work even in patt for 10 rows.

Bind off all sts.

Button Placket:
With right side facing you and with larger size needles, pick up 42 (50, 52) sts along center front opening.

Row 1 (wrong side):
* P1, K1; rep from * across.

Row 2 (right side):
* K1, P1; rep from * across.

Rows 2 through 5:
Rep Rows 1 and 2 twice.

Bind off all sts in patt.

Back
With larger size needles, cast on 76 (88, 100) sts. Change to smaller size needles.

Ribbing:
Row 1 (right side):
* K1, P1; rep from * across.

Row 2:
* P1, K1; rep from * across.

Rows 3 through 6:
Rep Rows 1 and 2 twice.

Change to larger size needles.

Body:
Row 1:
(K4, P2) 2 (2, 3) times; place marker; P2, K8, P2; place marker; (K4, P2) 4 (6, 6) times; K4; place marker; P2, K8, P2; place marker; (K4, P2) 2 (2, 3) times.

Row 2:
(K2, P4) 2 (2, 3) times; K2, P8, K2, (K2, P4) 4 (6, 6) times; K2, P2, K2, P8, K2, (K2 P4) 2 (2, 3) times.

Row 3:
(K4, P2) 2 (2, 3) times; P2, CB; CF; P2, (K4, P2) 4 (6, 6) times; K4, P2, CB; CF; P2, (K4, P2) 2 (2, 3) times.

Row 4:
Rep Row 2.

continued

Row 5:
K2, (P2, K4) 1 (1, 2) times; P2, K2, P2, K8, P2, K2, (P2, K4) 4 (6, 6) times; P4, K8, P2, K2, (P2, K4) 1 (1, 2) times; P2, K2.

Row 6:
P2, (K2, P4) 1 (1, 2) times; K2, P2, K2, P8, K2, P2, (K2, P4) 4 (6, 6) times; K4, P8, K2, P2, (K2, P4) 1 (1, 2) times; K2, P2.

Row 7:
K2, (P2, K4) 1 (1, 2) times; P2, K2, P2, CF; CB; P2, K2, (P2, K4) 4 (6, 6) times; P4, CF; CB; P2, K2, (P2, K4) 1 (1, 2) times; P2, K2.

Row 8:
Rep Row 6.

Row 9:
(P2, K4) 2 (2, 3) times; P2, K8, P2, (P2, K4) 4 (6, 6) times; P2, K2, P2, K8, P2, (P2, K4) 2 (2, 3) times.

Row 10:
(P4, K2) 2 (2, 3) times; K2, P8, K2; (P4, K2) 4 (6, 6) times; P4, K2, P8, K2, (P4, K2) 2 (3, 3) times.

Row 11:
(P2, K4) 2 (2, 3) times; P2, CB; CF; P2, (P2, K4) 4 (6, 6) times; P2, K2, P2, CB; CF; P2, (P2, K4) 2 (2, 3) times.

Row 12:
Rep Row 10.

Row 13:
(K4, P2) 2 (2, 3) times; P2, K8, P2, (K4, P2) 4 (6, 6) times; K4, P2, K8, P2, (K4, P2) 2 (2, 3) times.

Row 14:
Rep Row 2.

Row 15:
(K4, P2) 2 (2, 3) times; P2, CF; CB; P2, (K4, P2) 4 (6, 6) times; K4, P2, CF; CB; P2, (K4, P2) 2 (2, 3) times.

Row 16:
Rep Row 2.

Rows 17 and 18:
Rep Rows 5 and 6.

Row 19:
K2, (P2, K4) 1 (1, 2) times; P2, K2, P2, CB; CF; P2, K2, (P2, K4) 4 (6, 6) times; P4, CB; CF; P2, K2, (P2, K4) 1 (1, 2) times; P2, K2.

Row 20:
Rep Row 6.

Rows 21 and 22:
Rep Rows 9 and 10.

Row 23:
(P2, K4) 2 (2, 3) times; P2, CF; CB; P2, (P2, K4) 4 (6, 6) times; P2, K2, P2, CF; CB; P2, (P2, K4) 2 (2, 3) times.

Row 24:
Rep Row 10.

Rep Rows 1 through 24 three times.

Rep Rows 1 through 4 (8, 12) once.

Bind off next 24 (28, 32) sts; for neckline, * K1, P1; rep from * 13 (14, 17) times more; bind off rem sts.

Slip 28 (30, 36) neckline sts onto a stitch holder.

Sew shoulder seams, matching cables.

Neckline Ribbing:
Beg at center right front buttonhole placket, with right side facing you and smaller size needles, pick up 26 sts along right front neck edge; knit back neckline sts from holder, pick up 26 sts along left front neck edge—80 (82, 88) sts.

Row 1 (wrong side):
* P1, K1; rep from * across.

Row 2 (right side):
* K1, P1; rep from * across.

Rep Rows 1 and 2 three times.

Loosely bind off in patt.

Sleeve (make 2)
Ribbing:
With larger needles, cast on 36 (38, 44) sts. Change to smaller needles.

Row 1 (right side):
* K1, P1; rep from * across.

Row 2:
* P1, K1; rep from * across.

Rows 3 through 6:
Rep Rows 1 and 2 twice, inc 12 (10, 16) sts evenly spaced across last row—48 (48, 60) sts.

Change to larger size needles.

Body:
Row 1:
(K4, P2) 3 (3, 4) times; place marker; P2, K8, P2; place marker; (K4, P2) 3 (3, 4) times.

Row 2:
(K2, P4) 3 (3, 4) times; K2, P8, K2, (K2, P4) 3 (3, 4) times.

Row 3:
(K4, P2) 3 (3, 4) times; P2, CB; CF; P2, (K4, P2) 3 (3, 4) times.

Row 4:
Rep Row 2.

Row 5:
K2, (P2, K4) 2 (2, 3) times; P2, K2, P2, K8, P2, K2, (P2, K4) 2 (2, 3) times; P2, K2.

Row 6:
P2, (K2, P4) 2 (2, 3) times; K2, P2, K2, P8, K2, P2, (K2, P4) 2 (2, 3) times; K2, P2.

Row 7:
K2, (P2, K4) 2 (2, 3) times; P2, K2, P2, CF; CB; P2, K2, (P2, K4) 2 (2, 3) times; P2, K2.

Row 8:
Rep Row 6.

Row 9:
(P2, K4) 3 (3, 4) times; P2, K8, P2, (P2, K4) 3 (3, 4) times.

Row 10:
(P4, K2) 3 (3, 4) times; K2, P8, K2, (P4, K2) 3 (3, 3) times.

Row 11:
(P2, K4) 3 (3, 3) times; P2, CB; CF; P2, (P2, K4) 3 (3, 4) times.

Row 12:
Rep Row 10.

Row 13:
(K4, P2) 3 (3, 4) times; P2, K8, P2, (K4, P2) 3 (3, 4) times.

Row 14:
Rep Row 2.

Row 15:
(K4, P2) 3 (3, 4) times; P2, CF; CB; P2, (K4, P2) 3 (3, 4) times.

Row 16:
Rep Row 2.

Rows 17 and 18:
Rep Rows 5 and 6.

Row 19:
K2, (P2, K4) 2 (2, 3) times; P2, K2, P2, CB; CF; P2, K2, (P2, K4) 2 (2, 3) times; P2, K2.

Row 20:
Rep Row 6.

Rows 21 and 22:
Rep Rows 9 and 10.

Row 23:
(P2, K4) 3 (3, 4) times; P2, CF; CB; P2, (P2, K4) 3 (3, 4) times.

Row 24:
Rep Row 10.

Rep Rows 1 through 24, 2 (3, 3) times.

Small Size Only:
Rep Rows 1 through 8.

Bind off all sts.

Medium Size Only:
You have completed the back.

Bind off all sts.

Large Size Only:
Rep Rows 1 through 4.

Bind off all sts.

Finishing

Step 1:
Sew sleeves to sweater, matching centers of cables to shoulder seams.

Step 2:
Sew sleeve and side seams.

Step 3:
Sew buttons opposite buttonholes. Weave in all ends.

Hat Instructions

Cuff
Cast on 84 sts.

Row 1 (right side of cuff):
* K1, P1; rep from * across.

Row 2:
* P1, K1; rep from * across.

Rep Rows 1 and 2 until cuff measures 4", ending by working a Row 1.

Crown
Row 1 (right side):
* K4, P2; rep from * across.

Row 2:
* K2, P4; rep from * across.

Rows 3 and 4:
Rep Rows 1 and 2.

continued

Row 5:
K2, P2; * K4, P2; rep from * to last 2 sts; K2.

Row 6:
P2, K2; * P4, K2; rep from * to last 2 sts; P2.

Rows 7 and 8:
Rep Rows 5 and 6.

Row 9:
* P2, K4; rep from * across.

Row 10:
* P4, K2; rep from * across.

Rows 11 and 12:
Rep Rows 9 and 10.

Rep Rows 1 through 12 four times.

Rep Rows 1 through 6 once.

Shaping
Row 1:
* K2 tog; P2, K2; rep from * across—70 sts.

Row 2:
P2, K2; * P3, K2; rep from * to last st; P1.

Row 3:
* P1, K2 tog; K2; rep from * across—56 sts.

Row 4:
* P3, K1; rep from * across.

Row 5:
* P2 tog; K2 tog; rep from * across—28 sts.

Row 6:
* P1, K1; rep from * across.

Row 7:
* K2 tog; rep from * across—14 sts.

Cut yarn, leaving a 24" end.

Thread yarn end into tapestry needle and draw through all sts. Draw up tightly and fasten securely.

Finishing
Weave side seam carefully matching rows. Weave in all ends. Turn cuff upward.